THE POLITICS OF **EXILE**

THE **POLITICS** OF **EXILE**

Ideology in Henry James,

F. Scott Fitzgerald, and

James Baldwin

BRYAN R. WASHINGTON

Northeastern University Press / Boston

Northeastern University Press

Copyright 1995 by Bryan R. Washington

Library of Congress Cataloging-in-Publication Data

Washington, Bryan R.
   The politics of exile : ideology in Henry James, F. Scott
Fitzgerald, and James Baldwin / Bryan R. Washington.
      p.   cm.
   Includes bibliographical references.
   ISBN 1–55553–209–8
   1. American fiction—Europe—History and criticism.
2. Fitzgerald, F. Scott (Francis Scott), 1896–1940—Political and
social views.   3. James, Henry, 1843–1916—Political and social
views.   4. Baldwin, James, 1924–   —Political and social views.
5. Politics and literature—Europe—History—20th century.
6. American fiction—20th century—History and criticism.
7. Political fiction, American—History and criticism.   8. American
literature—European influences.   9. Exiles' writings—History and
criticism.   10. Exiles in literature.   I. Title.
PS159.E85W37   1995
818'.5409—dc20   94-27077

Designed by David den Boer of Nighthawk Design

Composed in Weiss by Coghill Composition Company in Richmond, Virginia. Printed and bound by The Maple Press Company in York, Pennsylvania. The paper is Sebago, an acid-free sheet.

MANUFACTURED IN THE UNITED STATES OF AMERICA

99   98   97   96   95   5   4   3   2   1

For **Sophia,** for **Joseph,** and for **Russell**

CONTENTS

The Politics of Exile

Introduction: The Discourse of Exile   3

1   Going to Meet the Master ("Going to Meet the Man")   17

White Flight

2   The Daisy Chain: *The Great Gatsby* and *Daisy Miller*
     or The Politics of Privacy   35

3   "Communities" of Exiles: *Tender Is the Night*   55

4   The Beast in *Giovanni's Room*   70

Strangers in the Village

5   Stranger's Return   95

6   Writing the American Scene: James and Baldwin,
     James/Baldwin, James Baldwin   109

7   In *Another Country*   127

Notes   143

Select Bibliography 153

Index 163

ACKNOWLEDGMENTS

My thanks to the Ford Foundation for its generous support and to Lafayette College for granting me a year off. I am also indebted to Princeton University, and to Elaine Showalter in particular, for appointing me a Visiting Fellow.

Special thanks to Randall Knoper, Werner Sollors, and Arnold Rampersad for reading my work.

The Politics of Exile

INTRODUCTION

The Discourse of Exile

This book maintains that both as an essayist and, more importantly, as a novelist James Baldwin implicitly calls for new readings of two of his precursors: Henry James and F. Scott Fitzgerald. Narratives like *Daisy Miller, The Great Gatsby,* and *Tender Is the Night* (to name three) end up reproducing the very sociocultural confusion and turmoil from which they attempt and fail to extricate themselves and out of which Baldwin's project emerges. For even though he labors to move beyond their tradition, Baldwin inevitably falls within it—is indeed, in some senses, its captive. And thus I argue that *Giovanni's Room* and *Another Country*, for example, are responses, conscious or unconscious, to the textual legacy of white exiles. Read in Baldwin's light, it is James's ideologies, not his forms, that become the main concern. And this approach also makes Fitzgerald's investment in James's at times deeply buried political thematics abundantly clear. Yet criticism has frequently denied or concealed the intricate politics animating their work: conservative, even reactionary, when it comes to race, gender, and class—potentially subversive with regard to sexual desire(s).

Although today only the most right-wing readers of canonical texts would confess to an utter lack of interest in gender theory, even critics on the left express a resistance to the figuration of racial and sexual "minorities" when they contemplate the Master and, as we are usually given to understand, his exclusively white pupils. Precisely because I am concerned with what happens when one juxtaposes the mainstream with the marginal, I have chosen texts well known within several (and, regrettably, frequently discrete) discourse communities. In other words, those who specialize in mainstream American literature will find themselves on familiar ground in terms of the narratives selected. And those whose critical practice emphasizes African-American and gay literatures will consider the texts examined obvious choices. But my point is that in order to read for the multiple issues that exile inscribes we need an interpretive strategy that transgresses such boundaries.

In *Black Literature and Literary Theory*, Henry Louis Gates, Jr., asks whether black theorists necessarily read differently: "If the relation of black texts to Western texts is problematic, then what relationship obtains between (Western) theories of (Western) 'literature' and its 'criticism' and what the critic of black literature *does* and reflects upon?"[1] I have reframed the question: What do black readers of white literature reflect upon? In view of the rapidity with which some white theorists are now consuming black texts, it is worth mentioning that African-American critics have largely avoided the white canonical mainstream. We have done so out of complex motives entwining our urgent loyalty to each other with the persistent fear that we hardly have time to attend to "our own" material, let alone the literature of the Other. Since we have only just begun to make a theoretical difference within the profession, laying claim to territories already colonized is perhaps self-defeating. As Toni Morrison ultimately suggests in *Playing in the Dark*, there are in fact long-standing institutional barriers dissuading black intellectuals from undertaking such a project.[2] I discuss Morrison's essay at some length in Chapter 1, arguing that it wrestles with the same questions about the relation between

blackness and whiteness with which Baldwin struggled throughout his career.

In *The Second Black Renaissance*, the English critic C. W. E. Bigsby
argues that American exiles "of the nineteenth century were concerned with engaging the Europe of fact and myth; those of the
early twentieth century tended to see it as a backdrop against
which their frequently neurotic heroes and heroines enacted their
entropic lives."[3] If Henry James is among the writers Bigsby has
in mind when he argues for the historically grounded shift in the
figuration of Europe, then one wonders how he would read *Daisy
Miller* (1878). As I suggest in Chapter 2, James's novella ultimately
questions whether narrative can or should respond to post–Civil
War America. Although the tale is set in Switzerland and in Italy,
its obsession with Daisy's whiteness, not to mention the fact that
she and her family make their pilgrimage to Europe on a ship
called the *City of Richmond*, points toward more than a casual narrative interest in a country supposedly left behind.

As for the generation of exiles following James, Fitzgerald is a
representative figure. *The Great Gatsby*, which I also consider in
Chapter 2, was written largely in France, but since it is set in
America it may attest to Bigsby's point. My own reading of the
novel, however, sees it as a revision of *Daisy Miller*, reclaiming not
only Daisy herself but Winterbourne too. If, in other words, Nick
Carraway is Winterbourne reimagined, his explicit androgyny,
even his possible homosexuality, not only explains his obsession
with Gatsby but also uncovers James's homosexual subtext. This
buried homosexual thematic, however, braces texts attempting
cultural custodianship, trying for the preservation of white authority—which of course implicates the generative, the pro-
creative, the filial. And yet, paradoxically, the antireproductive
homosexual is valorized precisely because he cherishes the "civilization" said to be on the verge of extinction. And he struggles to
enforce the social boundaries and hierarchies written out in the
texts in which, finally, he plays a crucial role.

Edward Said argues that in a reified world, where "natural relationships [are] virtually impossible," the affiliative rather than the filiative structures human social bonds. Referring specifically to high modernism, he reminds us that

> childless couples, orphaned children, aborted childbirths, and unregenerately celibate men and women populate . . . [that] world . . . with remarkable insistence, all of them suggesting the difficulties of filiation. But no less important in my opinion is the second part of the pattern, which is immediately consequent upon the first, the pressure to produce new and different ways of conceiving human relationships. For if biological reproduction is either too difficult or too unpleasant, is there some other way by which men and women can create social bonds between each other that would substitute for those that connect members of the same family across generations?[4]

White American exiles, figural (cultural) orphans yearning for the embrace of Europe, are similarly preoccupied—producing narratives in which celibates and euphemistic bachelors abound.

Certainly, homosexuality is central to Baldwin's work as well, but his homosexuals are not called upon to enforce boundaries and hierarchies, as is the case with James and Fitzgerald, but instead to break them down. As I argue in Chapter 7, this is what happens in *Another Country*. Eric's relationship with the French Yves can be understood as the articulation of that smooth blending of the Old World with the New that James calls for.[5] But Eric also has sexual relationships with a heterosexual married woman and with a bisexual black man. Binarisms of race and sexual orientation, then, are effectively collapsed. *Giovanni's Room*, the focus of Chapter 4, foregrounds yet another white homosexual whose anxiety about his sexual identity is at its most acute in Paris. But the way David persecutes other homosexuals, including his lover Giovanni, is associated with the persecution of African

Americans from the very beginning of the text. The boundary beween whiteness and blackness is once again transgressed. And, at the same time, so is the textual demarcation between Baldwin and James. For *Giovanni's Room* homoeroticizes "The Beast in the Jungle." But the figure of the male-male relationship in Baldwin's work is complicated by more than race as such. In this novel, and possibly in "Stranger in the Village" as well (which I discuss in Chapter 5), homosexuality suggests the impossibility not only of establishing kinship with the traditions of the West but also of reestablishing a cultural bond with Africa.

Claiming that black writers have always been "influenced" by white writers, Bigsby argues that this is particularly true of black exiles: "[T]he countries they chose, primarily France and Spain, were the countries which other writers had chosen. The France of Camus and Sartre drew the black writer for many of the same reasons which had attracted Hemingway, Fitzgerald, and Stein."[6] How can this be? Hemingway, Fitzgerald, and Stein were free in America. Moreover, on the evidence of their work, white exiles imagined Europe as the place where they could be free of black people. But in writing America against the "backdrop" of Europe, they acknowledged blackness if only by banishing it, so methodically, from the discursive scene. Claude McKay, Jessie Fauset, and Nella Larsen, not to mention Baldwin and Wright, denied basic rights in America, imagined Europe as the place where they could be free.

In the end, what most disturbs Bigsby about black exiles is that, like their white contemporaries, they too were disinclined to see Europe as a subject for narrative:

> What is striking . . . is the almost complete absence of interest in Europe as such. . . . For Wright, Baldwin, and Smith, it virtually disappears altogether. It is present, of course, in *Giovanni's Room*. But this is not so much a real Europe as an image of implacable determinism, which is the closest analogy to racial imperatives

which Baldwin can find outside of a homosexuality which is itself part metaphor. Europe simply does not feature. The eye remains securely focused on America.[7]

All this confuses. Apparently, black exiles should have gone elsewhere, because presumably elsewhere they would have been able to write themselves out of white traditions. But since they generally went to Europe, Europe should have been the focus of their work. The fact that black exiles—in this case Baldwin—chose to follow in the footsteps of whites (in their work and in their lives) is to Bigsby a paradox. Like so many white critics, he discounts the enormous weight white experience and white texts bring to bear on black experience and black texts. Because we are talking about black exiles, he implies, their blackness should have taken them to Africa, Jamaica, South America. And what would the textual result have been? In other words, how does one define blackness and the texts it produces? The inability to rescue blackness from whiteness is Baldwin's dilemma in "Stranger in the Village."

The classic study of twentieth-century American exile, Malcolm Cowley's *Exile's Return*, foregrounds the lives of the writers it surveys. Their texts are an ancillary concern. A self-congratulatory attestation to America's ability to come to its senses, to make room for rebels with or without causes, this in the final analysis is the story of repatriation rather than exile. For Cowley's exiles did indeed *return* to America, where they eventually found a home: if not within the culture at large, then certainly within the academy. But the writers who arguably owe their canonical success to a critical study that has become a classic in itself insisted in work after work that America was uninhabitable—uninhabitable for reasons Cowley systematically ignored. Both observer of and participant in his own tale, Cowley's ostensible historical "odyssey" is personal narrative.

Early-twentieth-century American writers, he claims, went to

Europe in droves because "[there] one was free to live and write in one's own fashion. . . . [There] one could lie abed all day and work through the night—or, if one chose, get roaring drunk, smoke hashish, sleep with the native girls, indulge in any sort of orgy without fearing the police or even public censure."[8] An exile, in short, is finally little more than a hedonist. To the extent that *Exile's Return* argues that those writers who lived abroad in the years between the wars were oblivious to politics, it is ironic that Fitzgerald, whose "novels and stories," we are told, "are in some ways the best record" of the 1920s and 1930s,[9] produced work so unambiguously concerned with America's cultural and social disintegration.

I have suggested that Fitzgerald co-opts and recontextualizes James's primary preoccupations. Among these are the extent to which the American female can civilize the American male, the notion of America as a land of innocents in need of an experience available only in Europe, and the paradoxical reverence for capital coupled with the absolute dismissal of capitalism. Although even today few critics make this point, these were essentially antidemocratic writers who feared the social consequences of blurred class boundaries: the direct result, they maintained, of America's fervor for industrialization and for urban expansion. Finally, particularly in their late work, the coming obliteration of the Anglo-Saxon became the emphasis. James, for example, despaired at the ubiquitous presence in America of Jews in particular and of the southern and eastern European working classes in general; arguably, he came to lament the emancipation of the slaves as well. Fitzgerald declared war not only on white "ethnics" but also on African Americans.

Of course, more recent work revises Cowley by focusing on the writers he ignores, namely, women and the African-American novelists and poets (male and female) living and writing in Europe during the period with which he is concerned. Shari Benstock's *Women of the Left Bank,* Mary Lynn Broe and Angela Ingram's *Wom-*

en's Writing in Exile, and Michel Fabre's *La Rive Noire* are among the most illuminating studies. My own objections to these investigations, however, stem from their tendency to marginalize further the "marginal" figures examined.

But the scholarship from which I would especially like to distinguish this book is encyclopedic rather than interpretive. Humphrey Carpenter's *Geniuses Together* is in essence, as the author himself admits, "a collage of Left-Bank expatriate life as it was experienced by the Hemingway generation—the Lost Generation, as Gertrude Stein named them in a famous remark to Hemingway."[10] Though Carpenter's "prologue" begins with Benjamin Franklin and ends with Henry James, his "main narrative," a jaunty account of what Americans saw and did in Paris from 1921 to 1928, revalorizes James's idea of Paris, and of Europe in general, as "a denser civilization than our own."[11]

In *Sylvia Beach and the Lost Generation,* Noel Riley Fitch sees early-twentieth-century American exiles as a motley crew bound together by Beach's lifelong commitment to publishing the work of the avant-garde. Harold McCarthy, in *The Expatriate Perspective,* casts a wide net, surveying not only the work of Cooper, Melville, Hawthorne, and James but also that of Richard Wright and Baldwin. The emphasis is on their differences rather than their common link, namely, their texts.

This question informs my thinking: If, as Wallace Martin argues, the novel is itself an exile (in the sense that it "opposes itself to the rules that are characteristic of other genres and 'poetics'"),[12] then is it significant that exiled writers, outsiders themselves, so often gravitated to this genre? In their formal properties, Fitzgerald's and James's narratives are frequently subversive, radical. But the implicit desire for, among other things, a racially monolithic society is resoundingly conservative. In Baldwin's work the reverse seems to be true: the politics is radical, while the structure is classic. In this material, then, form and ideology are at war.

Ernest Earnest's *Expatriates and Patriots* is the most comprehensive survey of American exile to date. In addition to novelists and poets, it also considers painters, musicians, and academics (although the experience of Harlem Renaissance writers is conspicuously absent). Earnest argues that the exile of "Hemingway, Fitzgerald, MacLeish, and Cowley . . . , like that of Cooper or Hawthorne, becomes little more than a footnote in a critique of their writings."[13] And thus he concludes that these writers, all of whom are now regarded as literary and/or critical authorities, are transcendent. But what of the America subsumed into their texts?

Cowley's intellectual contemporaries, including Fitzgerald, essentially reiterated his assessment of the American literary exile in their own memoirs. In *Paris Was Our Mistress*, for example, Samuel Putnam confesses that when he and his wife finally arrived in Paris, having resolved to live there forever, they fell down on their knees and wept:

> What my wife and I were experiencing in the moonlit Tuileries that first night was the beginning of a deep ingrowing love for a city and a land that were not ours, a love which every true "expatriate" felt and which came to be inextricably and more or less inarticulately intertwined with the reasons that he gave himself or others for leaving America or for staying on in France.[14]

Weeping in the Jardin de Tuileries by moonlight is an unhappy, indeed an embarrassing, image, one that prompted Harold Cruse to argue in *The Crisis of the Negro Intellectual* that Putnam's book is paradigmatic because its unabashed romanticization of Europe masks the politics motivating the so-called lost generation. As Cruse suggests, readings sensitive to what is only implied in their work reveal that white exiles writing between the wars saw themselves as "wide open for invasion by other culturally impure ethnic groups. . . ."[15] Fleeing to the Old World, they in effect took American literature with them. But the evacuation was as much a failure as James's had been a generation before.

The emotionality, the cloying nostalgia pervading memoirs like Putnam's is unrestrained in Fitzgerald's own meditation. In *The Crack-Up* Fitzgerald both declares himself an exile and appropriates the discourse of exile. In this posthumous volume of autobiographical essays, the European polis is opposed to the American metropolis. America is conceived as the enemy of the artist and of art itself. Women, allegorized, are represented as potential stabilizing forces in a textual phantasmagoria. And in the title piece, the "secret yen for . . . Scandinavian blondes" is the desire for the purest whiteness attainable undisguised. For the "sight of Celts, English, Politicians, Strangers, Virginians, Negroes (light and dark)" is intolerable.[16]

This, generally, is the ideology of James's *American Scene*, in which, as I suggest in Chapter 6, the successive images of flux and disintegration are among other things possible markers for race, for that is blackness. That *The Crack-Up* co-opts the Master's text becomes particularly clear when the subject is New York— imagined, as it is in James's "testimonial," as a spatial chaos. The city is "feverish" (26), "catering to dissipation" (30), "bloated, glutted, stupid with cake and circuses" (31). "As the toiler must live in the city's belly," Fitzgerald writes, "so I was forced to live in its disordered mind" (31). Digging into New York's past, his past, Fitzgerald tells us that in 1920 he was unable to identify a point of convergence: "Finding no nucleus to which we could cling, we became a small nucleus ourselves and gradually fitted our disruptive personalities into the contemporary scene of New York" (27).

For Fitzgerald, even art, or what passes for art, provides no possibility of stability because it too has been reified. D. W. Griffith's Long Island film studio, for example, manufacturing dreams for the masses, is in this text both symptomatic of the general chaos and somehow responsible for it: "[L]ater I realized that behind much of the entertainment that the city poured forth into the nation there were only a lot of lost and lonely people. The world of the picture actors was like our own in that it was in New

York and not of it. It had little sense of itself and no center" (28). "I saw that the novel," he continues,

> which at my maturity was the strongest and supplest medium for conveying thought and emotion from one human being to another, was becoming subordinated to a mechanical and communal art that, whether in the hands of the Hollywood merchants or Russian idealists, was capable of reflecting only the tritest thought, the most obvious emotion. (78)

The idea that part of Fitzgerald's dilemma as an exile involved the possibility that film had already supplanted or was about to overtake the novel is developed in Chapter 3. Arguing that it laments the dissolution of bourgeois hierarchies (not simply of art, but also of race, gender, and class), I focus there on *Tender Is the Night.*

I have suggested that Fitzgerald's female subjects are allegories, emblems of the distance between the ideal and the "real." Fitzgerald's men, on the other hand, struggle to maintain faith in the innocence of women, in their salvatory power. Such is the case with *The Crack-Up.* Fitzgerald explains that when he first arrived in New York he "interviewed a blowsy landlady in Greenwich Village. She told me I could bring girls to the room—why should I want to bring girls to my room?—I had a girl" (26). Even as a boy, he maintains, he saw women as goddesses: "When I was fifteen I went into the city from school to see Ina Claire in *The Quaker Girl* and Gertrude Bryan in *Little Boy Blue.* Confused by my hopeless melancholy love for them both, I was unable to choose between them—so they blurred into one lovely entity, the girl. She was my symbol of New York" (23). The transmutation of all women into one symbol of grace is the ostensible ambition of both *The Great Gatsby* and *Tender Is the Night,* insofar as they attempt to reclaim James's American "girl." But Fitzgeraldian reverence for women strikes a note of camp, as Susan Sontag might say, when it implicates theatrical performance.[17] Female sexuality, in other words, is frequently denied or defused in these texts, giving the effect of a narrative drag show.

In theorizing about the discursive outcome of reading *the* canon—specifically, the modernist canon—as an outsider, Houston Baker speculates that those who are "unconceived in the philosophies of Anglo-American, British, and Irish moderns . . . [will not] find intimacy . . . in their fawning reliance on an array of images and assumptions bequeathed by a *civilization* that, in its prototypical form, is exclusively Western, preeminently bourgeois, and optically white."[18] But Baldwin's work foregrounds the very intimacy that Baker dismisses. I am suggesting that the narrative desire to cling to the "optically white" West is to be found in texts coming well before and well after modernism and that it cuts across racial lines. Indeed, the idea that hallowed Western traditions are crumbling is arguably the point at which all narratives of exile intersect. Even though the historical event (the crisis) that precipitates exile (and its texts) is various, the insistence that the world (however defined) is falling apart, for whatever reason, remains the same. Still, Baldwin's reevaluation, as opposed to James's and Fitzgerald's revalorization, of Western traditions makes the signifying difference.

The readings emerging from this triangular configuration are not neutral. My own enunciative position is not unlike Baker's or, for that matter, Toril Moi's. In *Sexual/Textual Politics*, Moi raises her voice:

> I speak as a woman with only a tenuous foothold in a male-dominated profession. I also speak as a Norwegian teaching French literature in England, as a stranger both to France and to the English-speaking world, and thus as a woman writing in a foreign language about matters to which in many ways she remains marginal. Any marginalization is of course relative: I also speak as a white European trained within the mainstream of Western thought, which is why I feel that the issues raised by continental,

British and American feminism are still of crucial importance to my own critical and political practice.[19]

I am not a woman. I am, however, an African American wrestling as a teacher with the institutional and textual authority of the West. I am, like Baldwin, a marginalized, even an exiled, reader. In the courses that I teach in mainstream American literature, James and Fitzgerald cannot be avoided; teaching them is a canonical imperative. Still, my very marginalization conditions my approach to these writers and, I hope, to the way that white students (my typical audience) perceive what they take to be "their" literature, a field that of course also belongs to me. That is Baldwin's analogous position. For his work suggests that white texts are inescapable and that black readers must decide how to confront them. And thus Chapter 1, ultimately a reading of "Going to Meet the Man" (1965), supposes that the captive Baldwin freed himself simply by pronouncing the Master and his tradition his own.

Two years before he died, I asked Baldwin, then a writer in residence at the University of Massachusetts at Amherst, if he had come back to America to stay. He replied, as he so frequently did, "I'm a commuter."[20] The necessity of commuting to and from, of negotiating with white culture, informs what follows.

Going to Meet the Master
("Going to Meet the Man")

In his early work, Baldwin either invokes James—the Master—at the start or suffers his interruption. The second paragraph of "Stranger in the Village" (1953), for example, echoes the famous litany of America's cultural absences emitted in James's *Hawthorne* ("no Oxford, nor Eton, nor Harrow; no literature, no novels, no museums, no pictures, no political society, no sporting class—no Epsom nor Ascot!")[1]: "no movie house, no bank, no library, no theater. . . ."[2] The declamatory "Notes of a Native Son" (1955), as some have suggested, owes as much to James's *Notes of a Son and Brother* as it does to Wright's novel of protest. *Giovanni's Room* rewrites "The Beast in the Jungle." And "The Discovery of What It Means to Be an American" (1959) begins with a reference to the "complex fate."[3]

Even in work as comparatively late as *Another Country*, when Baldwin's career had been firmly established, James's presence is distinct. The novel's epigraph borrows from the preface to *Lady Barbarina*, in which James calls for a "sublime consensus of the educated," surmising at the same time that it will never occur: "They [Americans *and* Europeans] strike one, above all, as giving no account of themselves in any terms already consecrated by human use; to this inarticulate state they probably form, collectively, the most unprecedented of monuments; abysmal the mystery of what they think, what they feel, what they want, what they suppose themselves to be saying."[4] How, in short, do we or can we explain this iterative valorization of James?

In the late 1940s when Baldwin was avidly reading American literature in Paris, James had already been canonized. The House Un-American Activities Committee was at the height of its power, and the Master, arguably the first modern American literary exile, was newly important. He had not rejected the country; the country had rejected him, had rejected art. To the extent that James was embraced by an entire generation of intellectuals as dispirited as the so-called lost generation, Baldwin's following suit is hardly mysterious: nor is his decision to abandon America. Figuratively, Baldwin went to Europe to meet the Master, to claim for himself a tradition of dissent and departure. But this does not account for the readerly compromises he (must have?) made in order to locate himself, assuming that he could, in the Master's texts. Thus my interest in "Going to Meet the Man," the title piece in the collection of short stories Baldwin released in 1965. This text, I will argue, may in fact reveal that Baldwin's approach to James was less a question of slavish devotion than of systematic revision. For to meet "the man," the oppressor, is to confront and to challenge white authority.

Ian Bell has argued that "the formalism which James's fiction undoubtedly invites . . . requires readings which attempt to restructure it out of pure aesthetics in order to recognize the ruptures and difficulties of its historical occasions."[5] On the evidence of *The American Scene*, for example, approaches to James that move beyond formalism are imperative. In this late work, he speculates on the implications for America of the dissolving "Anglo-Saxon total," asking, "[W]hat meaning . . . can continue to attach to such a term as the 'American' character—what type, as the result of such a prodigious amalgam, such a hotch-potch of racial ingredients, is to be conceived of shaping itself?"[6] If such writing is representative, symptomatic of James's nativism and of his elitism, then why did Baldwin, by contrast a progressive, bother to read him at all?

Moreover, stepping away for the moment from James's work, there is the difficulty of the life itself: the privileges that his haute bourgeois whiteness guaranteed him. Born to a patrician intellectual family, James was educated in Europe as a matter of course. Baldwin, on the other hand, reared in poverty, was for a time a child evangelist whose frame of reference was confined to the ghetto. In terms of their formative years, not surprisingly, these writers are at opposite extremes of the social spectrum. Baldwin admitted that when he first read James he found himself grappling with a textual world virtually indecipherable to him. He told the biographer W. J. Weatherby that

> he had tried to read Henry James but hadn't got very far. James' elaborate sentences and the aristocratic European scene he described seemed completely foreign to him in Harlem. *The Portrait of a Lady* had been the novel he dipped into, and he still remembered the first sentence that had put him off: "Under certain circumstances there are few hours in life more agreeable than the hour dedicated to the ceremony known as afternoon tea." Said Baldwin: "It might have been a foreign language to me then."[7]

Having made a preliminary biographical stab at the issues problematizing Baldwin's dialogue with James and his disciples, I should point out that biography is not a resource to which I would ordinarily turn. Knowing full well that Fitzgerald's life of dissipation in the south of France was far different from James's genteel experience on the Continent and finally in England, the conclusion that Fitzgerald worked within James's tradition was nevertheless easily reached. The texts spoke for themselves. But

Baldwin's relation to James presents a different set of problems. Bloomian theories of influence, for example, because they ignore race and class, are unhelpful. Theories of intertextuality raise more questions in this context than they answer. Given the premise that the intertext is the textual unconscious, the critical project involves uncovering what has been repressed. But the co-optation of James that one remarks in Baldwin seems quite deliberate.

Is the very suggestion that Baldwin's blackness makes it difficult to understand what he could have possibly seen in James a function of racism in and of itself? Is race inevitably implicated in the construction of a readerly self? What is at stake here is the relevance of race (and class) when pondering who reads whom and why. After all, Baldwin himself frequently recoiled at the notion that his blackness was somehow a defining factor either in his career as a writer or (by implication) in his life as a reader. He notes in "The Discovery of What It Means to Be an American" that "I left America because I doubted my ability to survive the fury of the color problem here. . . . I wanted to prevent myself from becoming *merely* a Negro; or, even, merely a Negro writer."[8]

Three critics, in fact, who have attended to Baldwin's discipleship, if we can call it that, do not appear to have found it particularly troublesome. In "The Lesson of the Master," Charles Newman argues that Baldwin

> exploit[ed] social paradoxes, so it should not be surprising to trace his literary antecedents to neither Richard Wright nor Harriet Beecher Stowe, but to that Brahmin, Henry James. . . . The Atlantic Ocean separated James's mind into opposed hemispheres, and the gulf of color so cleaves Baldwin. The antipodes of their worlds propose a dialectical art. . . . Baldwin's characters suffer no more from their color than James's suffer from their money—these are only the peculiar conditions of their suffering. The problem for both is more universal—the opacity of their culture and the question of their identity within it. For Baldwin assumes, in the conse-

quence of his culture, the crisis of his identity, the reflective burden of Western Man. His color is his metaphor, his vantage . . .[9]

In *Stealing the Fire,* Horace Porter suggests that Baldwin looked to
James for technical and aesthetic guidance.[10] Porter's concluding
speculation: that in his determination to learn how James built his
house of fiction, Baldwin repressed his blackness. Lyall Powers,
chiefly a scholar of James, argues in his essay "Henry James and
James Baldwin: The Complex Figure" that the two writers have a
similar mission: "to examine the problem of learning to live in a
'civilized' society whose manners, conventions, prejudices often
threaten individual integrity; of coming to terms with that society's demands; and of managing to make the necessary compromises—but without giving up one's essential self."[11] Baldwin,
then, is a universalist for whom race, class, historical context, and
sexual orientation are ancillary concerns? Even the most cursory
reading of his work would reveal that this is not the case. And,
further, he consistently undermines the myth of individualism,
stressing the pervasiveness of cultural conditioning and pointing
out in the process that racism and, as Powers has it, civilized
society are mutually exclusive.

What critics have not noted is that Baldwin's development as a
writer occurred at precisely that point in American culture when
"great" writing was adjudged to be white writing. There was, in
fact, little else to read. The black writers of the nineteenth century whom Baldwin might have considered—in particular Charles
Chesnutt—were by the late 1940s virtually unavailable to the
general public, and certainly not to a young man from Harlem
hoping and ultimately obliged to "improve" himself, as a writer
and as a man, by mastering the masterworks of the West.

Embroidering on a concept that Du Bois lays out in *The Souls of
Black Folk,* Henry Louis Gates, Jr., has argued again and again that
African-American writers are split in two, that they are caught in
an acculturative double bind. Working within its institutions, its

political systems, its hermeneutics, they are compelled to learn how to communicate with the hegemony. Toni Morrison has recently raised the difficult question of why and how black readers (writers) negotiate with white texts. Claiming that she is "in awe of the authority of Faulkner's Benjy, James's Maisie, Flaubert's Emma, Melville's Pip, Mary Shelley's Frankenstein," she writes in *Playing in the Dark* of her interest "in what prompts and makes possible this process of entering what one is estranged from—and in what disables the foray, for purposes of fiction, into corners of the consciousness held off and away from the reach of the writer's imagination."[12]

Morrison's intellectual posture here is similar to Baldwin's in "Stranger in the Village," in which the "authority" of the West, its canons, dominates the discourse. Indeed, we might say that Morrison's career today mirrors Baldwin's at its apex. Her books critical and popular successes, she has an international reputation and a Nobel Prize. Yet despite her accomplishments, a frustration, even a sense of inadequacy, pervades *Playing in the Dark*. This is not to suggest that black writers are paralyzed by white writing, but rather that they must decide how to respond to it. The fact that such a decision has to be made in the first place distinguishes them from white writers, who are not deluged with blackness. White texts are everywhere. One response to their authority is to ignore it, a reaction that if fully articulated would involve ceasing to read most newspapers, academic journals, popular magazines, and books of any sort. It would also involve avoiding the bulk of theater, television, and cinema. Or one could simply capitulate to white textual authority, or subvert it, or retreat into one's own languages and literatures—assuming, of course, that they are discrete.

There is, however, another alternative. Since blacks are so thoroughly familiar with white cultural products, we may as well claim them for ourselves. Indeed, Baldwin frequently assumed the position of claimant. Morrison, on the other hand, questions the extent to which whiteness is knowable and therefore possessable. For her it is so wholly other as to be impenetrable: the "foray" into it is disabled. But why? Given that she herself demonstrates a substantial training in white texts, what obstruction interposes itself, prevents her from writing (imagining) whiteness?

Perhaps the stumbling block involves the internalization of an image of blackness (advanced in white texts) designed to neutralize the capacity to imagine oneself capable of writing at all. Morrison asks how much freedom she may finally have as an African-American reader and writer in a "genderized, sexualized, wholly racialized world,"[13] which is among the questions Baldwin posed—in infinite variations—all the time. Arguing that literary theory has avoided analysis of the figuration of blackness in white texts, Morrison pauses to consider the kind of scholarship that the Master himself has inspired:

> It is possible, for example, to read Henry James scholarship exhaustively and never arrive at a nodding mention, much less a satisfactory treatment, of the black woman who lubricates the turn of the plot and becomes the agency of moral choice and meaning in *What Maisie Knew*. Never are we invited to a reading of "The Beast in the Jungle" in which that figuration is followed to what seems to me its logical conclusion.[14]

Traditionally, of course, critics have responded to the Master's forms, as opposed to his ideologies. Even though the emphasis in the scholarship has begun to shift from poetics to politics, very little has been written on blackness in James because the interpretive community in question is largely conservative and white. Further, as I argue in Chapter 6, the fact that few have attended to the way blackness is figured (or is not figured) in James may be symptomatic of a desire to protect the Master and his texts from inquiries that would either marginalize his work *or* vulgarize it. It will become clear that the theoretical apparatus with the greatest potential for driving James away from the canonical epicenter emphasizes homosexual desire. And approaches foregrounding blackness invite the conclusion that James's genius for form masks a stunningly ordinary ideology about race.

Unfortunately, the focus of this book does not allow for the reading of *What Maisie Knew* that Morrison wants; however, I do address the extent to which blackness disrupts or penetrates the discourse in *Daisy Miller*. As for "The Beast in the Jungle," Morrison would seem to suggest that the figure of the jungle demands an approach sensitive to the way the text engages sexual repression by enforcing the binarisms of whiteness/blackness, civilization/jungle, and mind/body. If in fact this is the "logical conclusion" she intends, the reading she envisions could not avoid the homosexual thematics operating in the text as well. Indeed, the conflation of homosexuality and an implied blackness, as I shall indicate, is crucial to the revision of James's tale undertaken in *Giovanni's Room*.

White progressives have responded to *Playing in the Dark* with reservation. In her review of the book, Wendy Steiner, for example, argues that

> given the proliferation of African-American studies programs and, more generally, the politicization of literary scholarship, Ms. Morrison's charge that academics have ignored the topic of blacks in literature may seem surprising. At a time when conservative scholars and commentators are hammering the humanities for allegedly coercive political correctness, she can hardly fault criticism for reticence about race.[15]

The new visibility of black studies notwithstanding, Morrison implicitly questions the depth of institutional commitment to social reform. Steiner's underlying and dangerous white-liberal assumption is that because such programs are in vogue we now operate in a free marketplace of ideas from which racism has miraculously disappeared.

Morrison argues that as a novelist she, and by implication any black writer, is incapable of producing an authoritative whiteness. But, on the evidence of *Tar Baby* alone (in which white characters are central), one begins to wonder whether she is simply being playful or perhaps overstating her case in order to provoke us into reading white texts in new ways. For "Going to Meet the Man," a story we can be reasonably sure Morrison knows, organizes itself around and indeed invades a white consciousness. Since its point of view (third-person limited) is conventional, the text as a whole could be said to be faithful to the Master's forms. But the consciousness Baldwin constructs (one in which sexual performance, castration, homosexual repression, and miscegenation are clear and paralyzing concerns) voices what James either will not say or deliberately conceals. Finally, the narrative renounces Jamesian obliquity, unambiguously assaulting racial stereotypes by reproducing them: white people, cognitive, think about sex but are unable to engage in it; black people, unremittingly physical, are wholly defined by their sexual prowess.

Jesse is a white police officer attempting to enforce the racist status quo in a southern town during the climax of the Civil Rights movement, when young white liberals from the North were overseeing black voter-registration drives. At the beginning of the narrative, sex for Jesse, ignorant of himself but angst ridden, is merely a soporific. He caresses his wife, Grace, a "frail sanctuary":

> He stroked her breast. This was his wife. He could not ask her to do just a little thing for him, just to help him out, just for a little while, the way he could ask a nigger girl to do it. He lay there, and he sighed. The image of a black girl caused a distant excitement in him, like a far-away light; but, again, the excitement was more like pain; instead of forcing him to act, it made action impossible.[16]

Why the "image of a black girl" should simultaneously frustrate and enable sexual performance is the story's undergirding and unresolved dilemma.

If Jesse despises blacks, seeing them as "no better than animals" (231), he is also uncontrollably drawn to them, obsessed with them. What he wants to forget as he labors to fall into sleep, into unconsciousness, is the (cultural) police work he is obliged to perform. The story turns on an encounter he has had earlier in the day with a young black man, the alleged "ringleader" in the local Movement, who has resisted arrest. Cattle-prodded into submission, the protestor is ultimately jailed. Jesse's mission involves coercing the youth into mutiny, into disbanding his segment of the Movement, and, on a psychological level, into silencing the black and white protestors singing spirituals outside the jail. Their voices remind Jesse of the black mourners he had heard as a child as he made his way to his first lynching. Infiltrating the prisoner's cell, entering in effect what Baldwin calls in an essay of the same title "the male prison," Jesse applies his cattle prod to the young man's underarms and testicles. Brute force becomes a desperate sexuality:

> [Jesse's] mouth felt dry and his throat was as rough as sandpaper; as he talked, he began to hurt all over with that peculiar excitement which refused to be released. . . . He was glad no one could see him. At the same time, he felt very close to a very peculiar, particular joy; something deep in him and deep in his memory was stirred, but whatever was in his memory eluded him. (232–33)

"Whatever was in his memory" slowly emerges. The boy he nearly tortures to death is the grandson of "Old Julia . . . , a nice old woman" (234), one of his customers when he had worked as a payment collector for a mail-order house. In short, Jesse knows this young man. Years before he had once offered him some chewing gum. The response then: "I don't want nothing you got, white man" (235). Within the confines of the cell, Julia's grandson once again rejects what Jesse would proffer—namely, himself:

He began to tremble with what he believed was rage, sweat, both cold and hot, raced down his body, the singing filled him as though it were a weird, uncontrollable, monstrous howling rumbling up from the depths of his own belly, he felt an icy fear rise in him and raise him up, and he shouted, he howled, "You lucky we *pump* some white blood into you every once in a while—your women! . . ." Then he was, abruptly, almost too weak to stand; to his bewilderment, his horror, beneath his own fingers, he felt himself violently stiffen—with no warning at all; he dropped his hands and he stared at the boy and he left the cell. (235)

Having invoked "The Male Prison" (1954), a review of André Gide's *Madeleine*, I should say that its position on what Eve Sedgwick has called "homosexual panic" is directly applicable to "Going to Meet the Man," in which anxieties of sexuality and race are interdependent. Of the French novelist, Baldwin argues that "the two things which contributed most heavily to my dislike of Gide . . . were his Protestantism and his homosexuality. It was clear to me that he had not got over his Protestantism and that he had not come to terms with his nature."[17] Jesse is similarly repressed, similarly conditioned. On Baldwin's terms, he, and presumably all white men, will never free themselves, will never leave the cell, as long as white American culture insists upon denying its deeply rooted connection to black culture. As Baldwin suggests in "Stranger in the Village,"

At the root of the American Negro problem is the necessity of the American white man to find a way of living with the Negro in order to be able to live with himself. And the history of this problem can be reduced to the means used by Americans—lynch law and law, segregation and legal acceptance, terrorization and concession—either to come to terms with this necessity, or to find a way around it, or (most usually) to find a way of doing both these things at once. The resulting spectacle, at once foolish and dreadful, led someone to make the quite accurate observation that "the

Negro-in-America is a form of insanity which overtakes white men."[18]

Reconstructing the lynching he has repressed, Jesse remembers a childhood black friend: "His name was Otis. They wrestled together in the dirt" (240). But despite his admiration for Otis, who at the time "[h]e felt . . . knew everything" (243), Jesse was neverthelesss raised to believe that eight-year-old black boys mature into men who inevitably rape or want to rape white women. The ritual of the lynching is in Baldwin's hands reminiscent of "The Lottery," by Shirley Jackson—burning a black man alive, as with the annual stoning in her tale, is a routine atrocity. As Jesse's family joins the procession of whites making its way to the scene of the lynching, we are informed that "everyone look[ed] excited and shining, and . . . they were carrying food. It was like a Fourth of July picnic" (242). Indeed, Jesse's father pronounces the event just that—"a picnic" (243). And his mother, who "[h]e knew . . . wanted to comb her hair a little and maybe put on a better dress" (242), has time only to tie a ribbon in her hair that, en route to the killing, she "adjust[s] . . . , leaning forward to look into the car mirror" (244).

Baldwin's lynching derives its power from its point of view. The young Jesse is transfixed by the black male body itself, which is mythologized, written as massive, "big . . . and black as an African jungle Cat, and naked" (246). The genitalia are enormous: "huge, huge, much bigger than his father's, flaccid, hairless, the largest . . . he had ever seen till then, and the blackest" (248). Clearly, this is a sexual moment. Indeed, as Cornel West suggests in *Race Matters*, "everyone knows [that] it is virtually impossible to talk candidly about race without talking about sex. Yet most social scientists who examine race relations do so with little or no reference to how sexual perceptions influence racial matters."[19] More than twenty years ago, in the still illuminating *White Racism*, Joel Kovel made a similar claim, arguing that there is a mountain of evidence . . . to document the basically sexualized nature of racist psychology. Yet it is doubtful whether the majority of educated people have any idea of the extent, the organization, or intensity of such fantasies. Allegations as to the Negro's sexual prowess, or the heroic proportions of his genitalia, are a widely known legend. And it need scarcely be emphasized that discussions and speculations about Negro sexuality are neither casual and dispassionate nor uncharged.[20]

But Kovel, and more recently West, have little to say about how literature re-presents the tangled web of racism and desire. Perhaps no writer is more attuned to the "sexualized nature of racist psychology" than Baldwin. For it is precisely this issue that energizes so much of his work. In "Going to Meet the Man," we are never permitted to reach the safe conclusion that Jesse is unusual or aberrant. He is instead an average man, a typical racist. And yet the half-dead black man suspended from a tree is simply "the most beautiful and terrible object he had ever seen till then" (247).

"The archetypal lynching in the old South," as Kovel reminds us, "was for the archetypal crime of having a black man rape (= touch, approach, look at, be imagined to have looked at, talk back to, etc.) a white lady."[21] And of course, "the archetypal lynching often included a castration of the black malefactor; and even when it didn't, the idea of castration was immanent in the entire procedure."[22] In Baldwin's tale, even the castrating lyncher is figured a sexual predator:

> The man with the knife took the nigger's privates in his hand, one hand, still smiling, as though he were weighing them. In the cradle of the one white hand, the nigger's privates seemed as remote as meat being weighed in the scales; but seemed heavier, too, much heavier, and Jesse felt his scrotum tighten. . . . The white hand stretched them, cradled them, caressed them. (247–48)

The *jouissance*, the ecstasy, the castration releases in the crowd is both public catharsis and collective orgasm: "Then the dying man's eyes looked straight into Jesse's eyes. . . . Then Jesse screamed, and the crowd screamed as the knife flashed, first up, then down, cutting the dreadful thing away, and the blood came roaring down" (248). In "Going to Meet the Man" the climactic racial moment—the lynching itself—marks the beginning of Jesse's sexual "fulfillment." "Come on, sugar," he implores his wife, Grace, "I'm going to do you like a nigger, just like a nigger" (249). The great paradox of this white male heterosexual injunction is its context, one in which blackness and homosexuality, though anathematized, are finally unavoidable.

In so carefully foregrounding the sexual dynamics inherent in lynching, Baldwin may appear to have cast aside any allegiance to the genteel Henry James. On the other hand, in an interview published in the *Henry James Review* the year before he died, Baldwin argued against the commonly held view that "James had stayed in Europe describing, in effect, tea parties, while ignoring the most important event of the twentieth century, which was the American rise to dominance in world power. . . ."[23] When historicized, in other words, the Jamesian "tea party," the discourse of genteel exile, becomes politically charged. Citing *Daisy Miller, The Turn of the Screw, The Wings of the Dove, The Ambassadors, The Portrait of a Lady,* and *The Princess Casamassima,* Baldwin maintains that

> in each case [James] was describing a certain inability (like a frozen place somewhere) . . . to perceive others. So that Hyacinth, for example, in *The Princess,* is never a real person to the Princess. He's an opportunity for her to discharge a certain kind of rage, a certain kind of anguish . . . about why she's become the Princess Casamassima who had been Christina Light. . . . It seems to me that the Americans—unluckily for them—always have had a receptacle for their troubles, someone or something to pay their

dues for them. . . . The white American who only became a white American once he crossed the ocean . . . always had someone else to bear the burden for him: the Indian or the "nigger."[24]

Anticipating Morrison's *Playing in the Dark,* this remarkable analysis of James has implications not only for Baldwin's own project but for Fitzgerald's as well. The idea of the Other as a "receptacle for . . . [one's] troubles" is crucial both to *The Great Gatsby* and to *Tender Is the Night.* For these classics attempt to rescue white Americans (and narrative itself) from, as Baldwin puts it, the "nigger." The issue, then, is textual white flight.

White Flight

The Daisy Chain:

The Great Gatsby and *Daisy Miller*

or The Politics of Privacy

Beginning with the premise that *The Great Gatsby* revises *Daisy Miller*, the readings that I undertake in this chapter are concerned with various states of panic: sexual, racial, and social. Eve Sedgwick's theory of "homosexual panic," in other words, points toward a dense interpretive terrain extending far beyond, although always implicating, desire. As I have indicated, a repressed homosexuality undergirds "Going to Meet the Man." Moreover, it is associated with (or presented within the context of) racial discord. The idea that homosexuality and race are important for *The Great Gatsby* is hardly startling. Nick's fixation with Gatsby easily suggests flirtation, and his obsession with ethnic origins punctuates the text. But the notion that either homosexuality or race bears any relevance to James's novella may at first seem a critical anachronism.

Winterbourne, who frames the narrative, is a genteel conservator, even an enforcer. But in disciplining Daisy he responds to more than the defiant transgression of class boundaries that the time she spends with Eugenio (a courier) and Giovanelli (a questionable gentleman) represents. Published in 1878, *Daisy Miller* is not only the product of Reconstruction but also a commentary on the social (textual) implications of that era. Disembarking from the *City of Richmond*, Daisy arrives in Europe the incarnation of America after the Civil War, the unsuspecting emblem of "[c]ivilization . . . go[ne] to pieces."[1] The many references to her whiteness invite the speculation that whiteness is in serious jeopardy. But the insistence on whiteness prods blackness, in effect, into the text. Indeed, neither Winterbourne nor finally James can decide whether this new America, this Daisy, is educable, capable of understanding that, if blackness were to penetrate its discourse, James's narrative enterprise would cease to exist. Ignorant of the old textual rules, Daisy is dangerous. The threat she poses to the community of white American exiles imagined does not implicate only the potential assault of race. It also suggests the possible exposure of the homosexual underpinnings bracing not simply *Daisy Miller* but arguably all of James's texts. The effete Winterbourne, the suggestively asexual custodian of haute bourgeois conventions, is as necessary for the survival of James's genteel endeavor as the denial of blackness (or, for that matter, as Daisy herself). She, however, refuses to listen to him, refuses to be allegorized. Daisy prefers the company of comparatively manly men, who—by ushering her out of the drawing room (privileged in the text because it is so private) and through the streets to the public forum of the Roman Colosseum—quite literally put her at physical *and* social risk. His own narrative legitimacy in question, Winterbourne is almost desperate.

Equally (if less ambiguously) panicked, Nick Carraway valorizes the "Middle West"—

> not the wheat or the prairies or the lost Swede towns, but the thrilling returning trains of my youth, and the street lamps and sleigh bells in the frosty dark and the shadows of holly wreaths

thrown by lighted windows on the snow. I am part of that, a little solemn with the feel of those long winters, a little complacent from growing up in the Carraway house in a city where dwellings are still called through decades by a family's name. (177)

Ethnic cohesiveness and familial continuity are exactly the values James assigns to Europe. But the most persuasive indications of *The Great Gatsby*'s Jamesianisms are realized in the figuration of Daisy Buchanan, a woman of apparently irreconcilable dualities. Fitzgerald's Daisy is both a flower of innocence with the power to rescue Nick (and by implication Gatsby as well) from a com- modified world and a kind of cultural monster who betrays her creator's Romantic female ideal. As Nina Auerbach argues, "if the American Girl did not exist, James would have had to invent her as a personification of the United States. . . ."[2] Auerbach is con- cerned to show, and justifiably, that James's female subjects do not result from a steadfast feminism, but rather from the anticipa- tion of a "coming 'common deluge' that threatened to drown the private and fastidious perceptions of art," thereby making it pref- erable to pay lip service to the rhetoric of the "new woman" rather than endure "the garbage of mass lower-class culture that surged below her."[3]

James's American girl is an invention of narrative conceived to serve a particular cultural end: to halt the displacement of the rarefied, refined, and therefore feminine aesthetic world on which his vision depended by the aggressive, anti-aesthetic, and there- fore masculine world of commerce. In the sociohistorical sense, then, the female he portrays may have existed, but she by no means speaks for the whole of America—unless, of course, one assumes that the Americans who matter are white and rich. By contrast, the archetypal female whom Fitzgerald would reclaim *did* exist: she is the preoccupying force in James's most ambitious writing. The "fragment of lost words . . . uncommunicable forever" (112) is the textual past that Fitzgerald aims to recapture. Indeed, it will become clear that the critical work I draw upon, particularly in my discussion of *Daisy Miller*, is similarly invested. Lionel Trilling, William Wasserstrom, F. W. Dupee—all of whom were at their most influential in the 1950s—practiced a conservative readerly politics that contemporary critics generally revalorize.

In *Heiress of All the Ages*, William Wasserstrom sees James as the central figure in the genteel tradition, a tradition he defines as that group of texts concerned to "establish order within the human spirit and in the life of the society."[4] If, as Wasserstrom maintains, the genteel tradition strove to overcome the "vast distances of wilderness, religious disorganization, political disorder, slavery, Civil War, tenements, strikes,"[5] then the texts associated with it did so by attempting to remove themselves from them. Paradoxically, however, when the narrative scene shifts from America as such to Europe (imagined as stable) James's international fictions resonate with the tensions that made America the enemy of his narrative project. The genteel tradition saw democracy as antithetical to art. But, when it appropriated the novel—always new, always in process—as the primary vehicle of its message, it ultimately defeated itself: for the novel constitutes a democracy in and of itself. Few readers of *Daisy Miller*, however, have found solace in the dynamics of democracy animating it. F. W. Dupee, for example, considers Daisy's failure to listen to the voice of Europe intolerable, arguing that she is "a social being without a frame" who "does what she likes because she hardly knows what else to do. Her will is at once strong and weak by reason of the very indistinctness of general claims."[6] Similarly, Wasserstrom sees Daisy as "infantile," "ignorant"—a misguided innocent who "childishly throws away her life."[7]

To the extent that Daisy emblematizes the tension between America's impulse to democratize and Europe's compulsion to create hierarchies, the conflict is resolved only in her death. When Daisy sickens and dies, she is both silenced and, to invoke Bakhtin, "ennobled."[8] Wasserstrom argues that James saw the

American girl as the symbol of the "dream of history," as the heiress of a society that is the "heir of all the ages. It became therefore her duty to resolve and transcend all antitheses. When she failed, the result in literature was tragic. But when she brought off the victory, she paid the nation's debt to history."[9] Ideally, then, James's American girl permits the desired union between America and Europe. Her cultural assignment: to "achieve a great marriage in which two great civilizations would be joined."[10]

"Daisy and her mama," Winterbourne insists, "haven't yet risen to that stage of—what shall I call it—culture, at which the idea of catching a count or a *marchese* begins. I believe them intellectually incapable of that conception."[11] Though in the final analysis Winterbourne dismisses Daisy as an indecipherable text ("he soon went back to live at Geneva, whence there continue to come the most contradictory accounts of his motives of sojourn: a report that he's 'studying' hard . . .—much interested in a very clever foreign lady" [74]), his investment in shielding her from the scrutiny of other, potentially more invasive readers (suitors) is considerable. Daisy's conduct with her courier, Eugenio, suggests that she regards him as more than a servant. Indeed, Mrs. Costello pronounces their relationship an "intimacy," arguing that

"there's no other name for such a relation. They treat the courier as a family friend—as a gentleman and a scholar. I shouldn't wonder if he dines with them. Very likely they've never seen a man with such good manners, such fine clothes, so *like* a gentleman—or a scholar. . . . He probably sits with them in the garden of an evening." (17–18)

What is at risk here? The obvious response is that Daisy's crossing the conventional line between "mistress" and "servant" attests to her ineligibility as a genteel heroine. Which would explain Winterbourne's outrage at her ambiguously ardent relationship with Giovanelli, who on Winterbourne's terms is "a music-master or a penny-a-liner or a third-rate artist" (45). Were Giovanelli a member of the Italian nobility, were he for example Prince Amerigo of *The Golden Bowl*, then presumably he would be an appropriate suitor and a potential mate for Daisy, for America. But Daisy's transgressions implicate more than class. The emphasis on her whiteness, as I have suggested, is almost obsessive. At the beginning of the narrative she is "dressed in white muslin, with a hundred frills and flounces and knots of pale-coloured ribbon" (5). Indeed, references to her white dresses, white shoulders, white teeth crowd the text. This iterative whiteness, traditionally read as an affirmation of her virtue, is also simply—complicatedly—whiteness.

We know from *The American Scene* that James was greatly concerned that the country would never recover from the sociocultural split of the Civil War, but he also romanticized the antebellum South, which perhaps accounts for the name of the ship transporting the Millers abroad. Richmond, the capital of the Confederacy, is on the move, in transit. Why? Because white women and children must be evacuated? Implicitly, Daisy's archetypal whiteness is defined against its archetypal opposite, blackness. In short, since she blithely ignores class boundaries, would Daisy be capable of venturing further? Or, in the aftermath of the war, in the aftermath of the Emancipation, had America changed so irrevocably that anything could happen? As her conduct with Eugenio and Giovanelli invites us to speculate, Daisy would conceivably risk her own racial destruction were she permitted to pursue the implications of the social freedoms she embodies. This is what democracy does: it precipitates chaos. In James's tale, race is of course unspeakable. In *The Great Gatsby*, however, it dominates the discourse.

If Nick Carraway is Winterbourne unambiguously panicked, Daisy Buchanan is Daisy Miller fully recontextualized:

"You see I think everything's terrible anyhow," she went on in a
convinced way. "Everybody thinks so—the most advanced people. And I *know*. I've been everywhere and seen everything. . . .
Sophisticated—God, I'm sophisticated!" (18)

Assuming, then, that she is to reenact the drama of American
innocence, it is Daisy Buchanan's sophistication that prevents her
from fulfilling, as Wasserstrom would argue, her destiny. In *The
Great Gatsby* the figuration of women in general suggests an attempt to produce a suitable "heiress"—not of the ages, but to
the Jamesian legacy. Daisy (murderous cosmopolite) and Jordan
(innocent miller's daughter transcribed to dishonest baker's) are
genteel conspirators. But Myrtle, the potentially relentless force
in this gendered cultural garden, is expeditiously weeded out because she places male (textual) authority in even greater peril.

Like her namesake, Daisy Buchanan is defined by her whiteness. So is Jordan Baker:

The only completely stationary object in the room was an enormous couch on which two young women were buoyed up as
though upon an anchored balloon. They were both in white, and
their dresses were rippling and fluttering as if they had just been
blown back in after a short flight around the house. (8)

If these women can fly, then for Nick they are either angels or
witches, saints or sinners. In short, Nick is the prisoner of his own
classifications, desperately hoping that these privileged white
women are the female archetypes he needs them to be and hope-
lessly disenchanted when they prove to be more complicated
than his allegories of gender would allow.

Richard Godden suggests that Daisy has "repressed her body
and cashed in her voice, . . . described as 'full of money.' "[12] For
Godden, then, "the structure of Daisy's desire is economic."[13]
Myrtle, on the other hand, "is described most frequently in terms

of 'blood,' 'flesh,' and 'vitality.' "[14] (Her husband, Wilson, is represented as "blond," "spiritless," and "anaemic," as though his wife
has drained him of his vital fluids.) But that Myrtle, in contrast to
Daisy, is a woman who is entirely physical is not, as Godden
maintains, a function of her lack of commitment to "the production of manners" or to the trappings of the leisure class. Her New
York apartment, for example—"crowded to the doors with a set
of tapestried furniture entirely too large for it, so that to move
about was to stumble continually over scenes of ladies swinging
in the gardens of Versailles" (29)—strives to achieve the elegance
of Daisy's house on Long Island. Like everyone else in the novel,
Myrtle is a bracketed figure whom Nick "reveals" to us. The
woman he presents is literally Daisy in-the-flesh, ominous because of her social aspirations and because of her almost manly
sexuality.

Myrtle's purchases, made en route to the apartment that Tom
has procured for her, point up her ambition and her ignorance: "a
copy of *Town Tattle* and a moving-picture magazine, . . . some cold
cream and a small flask of perfume," and, finally, a puppy of an
"indeterminate breed" (27). This, then, is a woman who has yet
to learn the difference between mongrels and Airedales, between
gossip magazines and the social register. In a text preoccupied
with and intolerant of the racial and social hybridization of
America, Myrtle's most unforgivable sin is perhaps her inability
to distinguish a hybrid from a thoroughbred. Her lack of judgment applies not only to dogs but also, apparently, to men. Nick
reports that Myrtle married her husband because she thought "he
knew something about breeding, but," she adds, "he wasn't fit to
lick my shoe" (35). But Myrtle, of course, knows nothing of
breeding. The testimony of her narrow escape immediately follows her sister's narrative about an abortive affair with a Jew: "I
almost married a little kike who'd been after me for years. I knew
he was below me. Everybody kept saying to me: 'Lucille, that

man's way below you!' But if I hadn't met Chester, he'd of got me sure" (34).

And yet, always conscious of the boundaries he transgresses, Nick too is a nativist:

> As we *crossed* [my emphasis] Blackwell's Island a limousine passed us, driven by a white chauffeur, in which sat three modish negroes [*sic*], two bucks and a girl. I laughed aloud as the yolks of their eyeballs rolled toward us in haughty rivalry. (69)

His conclusion: "Anything can happen now that we've slid over this bridge, . . . anything at all . . ." (69). Nick's is the laughter of terror, for the black men he depicts have literally passed him by. The encounter, it seems, is so disconcerting that the overtaking passengers are denied voice.

In *Modernism and the Harlem Renaissance,* Houston Baker laments Fitzgerald's failure to place "his 'pale well-dressed negro' [the black man who identifies the car that kills Myrtle] in the limousine,"[15] suggesting that had Fitzgerald done so he would have acknowledged the legitimacy of the Harlem Renaissance—the black writers of the 1920s, many of whom were indeed "pale." He would, in short, have overturned the racial stereotype of black inarticulacy upheld in the text. Moreover, the presence of "pale-skinned" blacks confirms the worst fears of those who foresee the dissolution of Anglo-Saxon supremacy. For to be pale-skinned *and* African American is to be—like Myrtle's dog—a mongrel.

Nick's reaction to the blacks in the limousine recalls Tom Buchanan's unabashed racism:

> "Civilization's going to pieces. . . . I've gotten to be a terrible pessimist about things. Have you read 'The Rise of the Colored Empires' by this man Goddard? . . . Well, it's a fine book, and everybody ought to read it. The idea is if we don't look out the white race will be—will be utterly submerged. It's all scientific

stuff; it's been proved. . . . It's up to us, who are the dominant race, to watch out or these other races will have control of things." (13)

Though Tom misidentifies the author (the reference is to Lothrop Stoddard's *Rising Tide of Color against White Supremacy*, prominently displayed in Gatsby's library), his views are corroborated in the novel as a whole. Camouflaged in the discourse of the fall of civilization or of a remembered but unattainable past, Fitzgerald's subtext, to which Tom points, encodes a darker message. As Baker argues, Tom might be "a more honestly self-conscious representation of the threat that some artists whom we call 'modern' felt in the face of a new world of science, war, technology, and imperialism. . . . What really seems under threat are not towers of civilization but rather an assumed supremacy of boorishly racist, indisputably sexist, and unbelievably wealthy Anglo-Saxon males."[16]

Myrtle's ineptitude when it comes to identifying the breed of dogs or men equates with Nick's inability to determine who Gatsby is. Nick says of his mysterious neighbor: "I knew I had discovered a man of fine breeding after I talked with him an hour. I said to myself: 'There's the kind of man you'd like to take home and introduce to your mother and sister' " (73). As I shall demonstrate, this is an intricate textual moment. Arguably, it is at this point that Nick's readiness to welcome Gatsby to the nativist family, to extend a fraternal embrace, is at its most pronounced. Given his earlier reservations about his background, Nick's renewed conviction that Gatsby is indeed a "man of fine breeding" can be read as an ethnological sigh of relief:

> I would have accepted without question the information that Gatsby sprang from the swamps of Louisiana or from the lower East Side of New York. That was comprehensible. But young men didn't—at least in my provincial inexperience I believed they didn't—drift coolly out of nowhere and buy a palace on Long Island Sound. (49)

And thus when it is finally disclosed that Jay Gatsby is Jimmy Gatz and possibly more than merely casually connected with Meyer Wolfsheim ("a small, flat-nosed Jew" with tufts of hair in his nostrils and "tiny eyes" [69–70]), why Gatsby's ambiguous ancestry, his questionable past, is intolerable to Nick begins to make sense. To say that "Jay Gatsby of West Egg, Long Island, sprang from his Platonic conception of himself" (99) is to confirm that he is the worst kind of outsider. Gatsby, unlike Daisy and Tom (Nick's distant cousins), is of no relation. He is as much a threat to the "family"—to the "Middle West," to the white cultural center—as Myrtle, the "black bucks" in the limousine, or Wolfsheim.

But complicating the deliberation over bringing Gatsby home is desire itself. Does Nick speak as a man, a woman, or both? Like Eliot's Tiresias, Nick is "within and without, simultaneously enchanted and repelled by the inexhaustible variety of life" (36)—capable, that is, of being both male and female, Jew and gentile, black and white. Insofar as *The Great Gatsby* is indebted to *The Waste Land*, its commitment to salvaging whatever is left of "civilization" (as with poem) is articulated by one "in whom the two sexes meet."[17] The androgynous Tiresias bears witness to a culture in decline. He attests to the imminent demise not only of Europe (as text) but also of its institutions (implicitly the Church) and the strictly enforced hierarchies that fostered them. The "typist home at tea time" is an outrage and a devastation precisely because she is a typist—reductio ad absurdum of Philomel.

If Nick is like Tiresias, he is also like the sexually neutral Winterbourne. When he looks at Daisy, when he "stud[ies]" her, Winterbourne's gaze is not that of a potential suitor, but instead that of a decorous cultural chaperone searching for a charge who will behave. Fitzgerald's revision of James's tale foregrounds the deeper narrative implications of her misconduct. As I have pointed out, Myrtle is Daisy's déclassé double. Just as she is socially presumptuous, she is also physically overwhelming: her clothing "stretche[s] tight over her rather wide hips," and her figure is "thickish," "faintly stout." Nick observes that "she carried her surplus flesh sensuously as some women can. Her face . . . contained no facet or gleam of beauty, but there was an immediately perceptible vitality about her as if the nerves of her body were continually smouldering" (25–26). As Nick conceives it, Myrtle's sexuality is aggressive, masculine; her body authoritative. She is a match for Tom and thus a threat to Tom, who breaks her nose. Indeed, her "smouldering" presence is so disruptive that she has to be contained, locked up in Wilson's house. And when she breaks free, shouting "Beat me! . . . Throw me down and beat me, you dirty little coward!" she runs to her death. But killing her is not enough. Her "left breast . . . swinging loose like a flap [and her] mouth . . . wide open and ripped at the corners" (138), she is also mutilated, and her sexual power (in effect) neutralized.

There is an element of misogyny at work here that further problematizes the figuration of Nick. What values are assigned to him? Does the bald revulsion at female sexuality suggest homosexual panic? If it does, then *The Great Gatsby* affirms the cliché that for homosexuals women, appetitive and predatory, are terrifying. On these homophobic terms, Myrtle is loathsome because, defined only by body, she makes it impossible for Nick to romanticize male-female relationships, to see them as anything other than base, physical exchange. On the other hand, Nick's disgust with Myrtle is conceivably Winterbourne's frustration with Daisy laid bare. The stereotypical homosexual sensibility we confront, which James's work authorizes, is one repelled by a female figure whose gross ignorance and unfailing disobedience are the enemy of manners. Myrtle (desire incarnate) and Daisy (desire disembodied) are "monstrous doubles," and thus one of them must be sacrificed. In other words, René Girard's theory of myth and ritual is in this context quite useful. For Myrtle can be read as a "surrogate victim" whose death results (or is meant to result) in the restoration of order to the community.[18]

The Great Gatsby co-opts James's figure of the hotel as a "synonym" for America's social disintegration. As James said of the Waldorf Astoria, "one is verily tempted to ask if the hotel-spirit may not just *be* the American spirit most seeking and most finding itself."[19] Indeed, in *Daisy Miller* the social critique of the hotel, which "represents the abolition of privacy and decency,"[20] is buried in the discourse of the aesthetic. Describing the rooms the Millers have taken in Rome, Daisy defers to Eugenio, who considers them the best in the city. But the aesthetic judgments of an Italian courier are in James's hierarchicized world less than worthless. "Splendid" though they may be, these rooms are nevertheless public accommodation. Giving voice to the "mysterious land of dollars and six-shooters," Daisy's brother Randolph makes it clear that the Millers are accustomed to a superabundance of gilded space: "We've got a bigger place than this. . . . It's all gold on the walls" (37). Indeed, Daisy's mother's imagination is the captive of the hostelry: " 'I guess we'll go right back to the hotel,' she remarked with a confessed failure of the *larger* [my emphasis] imagination" (41). The cultural vision of Americans like these, then, is truncated. And yet the imaginative capability privileged in the text is smaller, not larger. The Millers are reproved for their attraction to the gigantic, the overstuffed, the overgilded, and the distinctly public. They are exhorted to narrow their scope, to exclude themselves from mass society—to be small.

When Daisy Buchanan decamps to her lover's house, Gatsby essentially shuts down the inn: "the whole caravansary had fallen in like a card house at the disapproval in her eyes" (114). In penetrating Gatsby's territory, then, Daisy is a potentially civilizing (privatizing) force:

> She was appalled by West Egg, this unprecedented "place" that Broadway had begotten upon a Long Island fishing village— appalled by its raw vigor that chafed under the old euphemisms and by the too obtrusive fate that herded its inhabitants along a short-cut from nothing to nothing. (108)

Gatsby's sprawling house (and by extension all that occurs there) repels because it is a phenomenon rather than a "place," an augury of things to come. It is a luxurious "roadhouse" to which all are admitted, a "factual imitation of some Hôtel de Ville in Normandy, with a tower on one side, spanking new under a thin beard of raw ivy, . . . and more than forty acres of lawn and garden" (5). The owner of this "colossal affair" is a kind of aesthetic criminal whose "art" Nick condemns—a reaction immediately undermining the reliability of a narrator who announces in the ninth line of the text that he is "inclined to reserve all judgments" (1). For, if nothing else, *The Great Gatsby* is a litany of judgments of the most reactionary sort.

In contrast to Gatsby's ersatz residence, Nick's "small eyesore" of a house is the ideologically privileged trysting place for Daisy and Gatsby. It is a model of privacy. Though, as Gatsby deduces, Nick "doesn't make much money," he is nevertheless perfectly capable of producing an afternoon tea that certifies his pedigree. Replete with lemons and lemon cakes and prepared by a female servant (unnamed, dismissed as "my Finn" [113]), the haute bourgeois tea that Nick serves to friends suggests that his house is a "home." The parvenu Gatsby, on the other hand, is host to endless caravans of visitors whom he does not know. Klipspringer, for example, is a permanent but unidentified guest—a visible indication of the social phantasmagoria Gatsby's way of life represents, as are the nightly parties themselves. Gatsby's guests are "swimmers," "wanderers," anonymous "groups [that] change more swiftly, swell with new arrivals, [and] dissolve and form in the same breath," "confident girls who . . . glide on through the sea-change of . . . men pushing young girls backward in eternal graceless circles" (41, 46). Gatsby's parties play out the "Jazz History of the World," the music Nick remembers from the first party he attends. Jazz is, in Nick's eyes, the music of commerce, its syncopations and rhythms, as Theodor Adorno argues, defined by the demands of the marketplace.[21] Indiscriminate, catering to the masses, jazz, in other words, speaks for Gatsby.

Matthew Bruccoli insists that "*The Great Gatsby* provides little in the way of sociological or anthropological data,"[22] which is another way of saying that its meanings transcend their historical context. Why dehistoricize the text? To safeguard its status as a "classic"? Consider, for example, the names of some of Gatsby's guests: Blackbuck, the Poles, Da Fontano, Don S. Schwartze, Horace O'Donovan, and the Kellehers. These clearly attest to Fitzgeraldian outrage at the new America, one in which so-called ethnics are ubiquitous—in which the citizens of East Egg, who form a "dignified homogeneity" in the midst of the "many-colored, many-keyed commotion" (45, 105), must contend not only with the inhabitants of West Egg but with all of New York.

"On week-ends . . . [Gatsby's] Rolls-Royce [later characterized as "swollen . . . in its monstrous length with triumphant hat-boxes and supper-boxes, and terraced with a labyrinth of wind-shield that mirrored a dozen suns" (54)] became an omnibus, bearing parties to and from the city between nine in the morning and long past midnight, while his station wagon scampered . . . to meet *all* [my emphasis] trains" (39). And ready to welcome the masses stands Gatsby—a fraudulent feudal lord in command of a serfdom of household staff charged with keeping the whole thing going: "on Mondays eight servants, including an extra gardener, toiled all day with mops and . . . garden-shears, repairing the ravages of the night before" (39). And "every Friday five crates of oranges and lemons . . . left his back door in a pyramid of pulpless halves. There was a machine in the kitchen which could extract the juice of two hundred oranges in half an hour if a little button was pressed two hundred times by a butler's thumb" (39).

The details of Gatsby's household evoke James's Newport "white elephants," the enormous "cottages" of the summering rich that in *The American Scene* have replaced the quaint abodes James knew in his youth:

[I]t was all so beautiful, so solitary and so "sympathetic." And that indeed has been, thanks to the "pilers-on-of gold," the fortune, the history of its beauty: that it now bristles with the villas and palaces into which the cottages have all turned, and that those monuments of pecuniary power rise thick and close, precisely, in order that their occupants may constantly remark to each other, from the windows to the "ground," and from house to house, that it *is* beautiful, it *is* solitary and sympathetic.[23]

The edifices that "rise thick and close" in Newport are in *Gatsby* faithfully reproduced: Nick's house is "squeezed between two huge places that rented for twelve or fifteen thousand a season" (5).

In *Slouching towards Bethelehem*, Joan Didion, also horrified by the crumbling of traditional values (although she attributes the erosion to the social upheaval of the 1960s), returns to James's Newport to report, quoting *The American Scene* almost verbatim, that "no aesthetic judgment could conceivably apply to the Newport of Bellevue Avenue," where "the air proclaims only the sources of money" and where "the houses [like Gatsby's] are men's houses, factories, undermined by tunnels and service railways, shot through with plumbing to collect salt water, tanks to store it, devices to collect rain water, vaults for table silver, equipment inventories of china and crystal and 'Tray cloths—fine' and 'Tray cloths—ordinary.' "[24] On these elitist terms, Gatsby's house is the quintessential male (public) bastion that presumably could be gentrified under the supervision of a woman like Daisy, whose taste Nick both endorses and replicates. The contrast, in fact, between Daisy's house and her lover's is striking: it is an architectonic utopia,

> a cheerful red-and-white Georgian Colonial mansion, overlooking the bay. The lawn started at the beach and ran toward the front door for a quarter of a mile, jumping over sun-dials and brick

walks and burning gardens—finally when it reached the house
drifting up the side in bright vines as though from the momentum
of its run. The front was broken by a line of French windows,
glowing now with reflected gold and wide open to the warm
windy afternoon. (6–7)

Daisy's house is not only a model of tasteful (though conspicuous) consumption, effortlessly marrying the best of Europe with
the best of America, and subtly enshrining a woman who has
"been everywhere and done everything." It also embodies the natural elegance associated with Daisy Miller—as though she has
finally forsaken the hotel. The Buchanan mansion is an extension
of the landscape surrounding it: "The windows were ajar and
gleaming white against the fresh grass outside that seemed to
grow a little way into the house. A breeze blew through the room,
blew curtains in at one end and out the other like pale flags,
twisting them up toward the frosted wedding-cake of the ceiling,
and then rippled over the wine-colored rug, making a shadow on
it as wind does on the sea" (8).

Gatsby's house, by contrast, is "unnatural," not simply because
of the way it imposes itself on the landscape or because of who
is invited there but also because of its interior. Rather than achieving a sanctified marriage with Europe, equated in East Egg with
nature itself, Gatsby's "palace" is represented as the product of a
cultural rape, as a kind of bastardized museum in which visitors
wander through "Marie Antoinette music-rooms and Restoration
salons" (92) unable to detect an organizing logic beneath the labyrinth of exhibits. The house is so clearly designed to accommodate the public that, during a private tour with Gatsby as guide,
Nick suspects that there are "guests concealed behind every
couch and table, under orders to be breathlessly silent until we
had passed through" (92). The most significant room, given what
it says about Gatsby, is the "Merton College Library" (92)—de
rigueur for a self-invented Oxford man: "we [Nick and Jordan]

tried an important-looking door, and walked into a high Gothic library, panelled with carved English oak, and probably transported complete from some ruin overseas" (45). Here a "middle-aged man, with enormous owl-eyed spectacles," exclaims that the books are "absolutely real—have pages and everything. I thought they'd be a nice durable cardboard" (45–46). They are not. The pages, however, are uncut. Gatsby, as untutored as Daisy Miller, does not read: his books are merely part of the inventory.

The novel's climactic scene unfolds in the Plaza Hotel. As though guests at one of Gatsby's parties, the principal players in the text are "herded" into a single "stifling" room—their private drama acted out in what is effectively a theater. Tom and Daisy's marriage is a corporate merger. Gatsby (the Arrow Shirt man) and Daisy (whose voice itself sounds like money) are equally commodified. The reified "personal" relationships and disintegrating traditional values Nick perceives are symptomatic of a country that for him, as for Fitzgerald, has become uninhabitable. "Nowadays," Tom says, "people begin by sneering at family life and family institutions, and next they'll throw everything overboard and have intermarriage between black and white" (130). Though Nick dismisses this outburst as "impassioned gibberish" (130), as the hypocritical response of a man who has suddenly transformed himself from "libertine to prig" (131), his own view of the American dilemma bolsters Tom's.

The celebrated concluding paragraphs of *The Great Gatsby* compose a reactionary social manifesto dressed up in the romantic rhetoric of loss. But a loss of what? Of innocence? Of the promise of spiritual perfectibility that the idea of America held out to its colonizers? As Baldwin suggests in "Stranger in the Village," the answer depends on whether, ancestrally, one is a conqueror or one of the conquered. Readers who are not descended from the "Dutch sailors" invoked may wonder at Lionel Trilling's depoliticizing and still largely unquestioned assessment of a writer now unavoidable: "the root of Fitzgerald's heroism is to be found . . . in his power of love."[25]

As it turns out, Daisy was always a discursive failure. In both narratives, women are exhorted to save "America," which is to say a particular textual tradition whose values and assumptions about what a culture should properly do and be are in jeopardy. Figuring America a cultural battlefield, James advocates evacuation, manning a textual lifeboat bearing the refugee of sanctified white womanhood. Awaiting Daisy stands the ultimately ineffectual Winterbourne, whose refined (homosexual?) sensibility, whose valorization of Europe (represented as the *only* culture) is crucial to James's work as a whole. However, Daisy's baggage, the conflicts of class and race with which — from the very beginning — she is ineluctably associated, proves too heavy; thus she is disciplined, and finally punished by death.

As an illustration of the sense of urgency underscoring the discourse of white American exiles, *The Great Gatsby* is clear enough. *Tender Is the Night*, however, to which I am about to turn, brings both Fitzgerald's social agenda and his ongoing dialogue with James into sharper focus. The opening paragraph, for example, depicting a hotel "on the pleasant shore of the French Riviera,"[26] is James's synonym for America invoked yet again. Gausse's Hôtel des Étrangers is isolated from its surroundings: bounded on all sides by mountain ranges, pine forests, "the pink and cream . . . fortifications of Cannes," and by the sea itself, where "[m]erchantmen crawled westward [i.e., to America, the land of commerce] on the horizon" (9). Inscribing a "littoral [cut off] from true Provençal France" (9) and populated by Americans as contemptible as the Buchanans, *Tender Is the Night* is a meditation on boundaries and thresholds.

Recalling James's nostalgia for the old Newport, Fitzgerald suggests that his Riviera was once a place of genteel beauty, where the "cupolas of a dozen old villas rotted like water lilies among the massed pines" (9) — was once untouched by the "pilers-on-of

gold." And there are further references to James—especially to
Daisy Miller. Geneva, Zurich, Vevey, the Swiss cities dominating
the map of Daisy's European experience, are Dick Diver's familiar
haunts. As with Daisy, his education begins in Switzerland, and
he also hails from the same American region. Daisy is from Sche-
nectady; Dick is from Buffalo. But in Fitzgerald's text, Switzerland
is more than the backdrop for a tragicomedy of manners drama-
tizing the differences between Europeanized Americans and paro-
chial patriots: it is "the true centre of the Western World" (167).

"Communities" of Exiles:
Tender Is the Night

Dick Diver arrives in Europe a man of illusions, "illusions of . . . the essential goodness of people; illusions of a nation, the lies of generations of frontier mothers who had to croon falsely, that there were no wolves outside the cabin door."[1] Clearly, this is a crucial moment: not only, it seems, is nationhood (and by extension filiation) illusory, but, in a text exhorting us to contemplate its romantic rhetoric of loss, so too is the consoling power of art. If art betrays us, then so presumably do women, who "croon falsely," whose capacity to nurture and protect is, like Gatsby's idea of Daisy as a woman of abiding love, a "colossal . . . illusion."[2]

As is so often the case in the discourse of exile, *Tender Is the Night* moves back in time, distancing itself from its reified "now" and ultimately recontextualizing the signal events of the nineteenth century. Beyond the reference to the romanticized frontier, there are allusions to the Civil War (in particular to Harriet Beecher Stowe), to the intractable presence in America of "ethnics," to imperialism, and to the apparently regrettable social consequences of industrialization. These "hard facts" pull at the text at every point,[3] revealing that it intends less to eulogize the old

Europe than to historicize America. Read in this way, *Tender Is the Night* becomes a novel of extraterritorial crisis, one in which the moorings of "civilization" have been severed, leaving Dick Diver at the helm of a boat as "drunken" as Rimbaud's.

If (for Fitzgerald) America is the potential prey of allegorical wolves, then who or what are they? I am about to suggest that white women (white women, that is, who have liberated themselves from the enclosure of the frontier cabin) and black men (who, no longer in chains, inevitably threaten the sanctity of white women) are among the hungriest predators in the pack. I am also concerned with the novel's commitment to maintaining hierarchies of class and art. For *Tender Is the Night* is a narrative of outrage and accusation, reproving the film industry for undermining the primacy of the novel and chastising the upwardly mobile working classes for daring to enter the drawing room. As will become clear, the prophecy of cultural doom is at its most pronounced in what I have called the Peterson episode, the "race riot" (112) that brings book one to its melodramatic close. In this section of the text—where Rosemary, a movie star (and by implication Nicole, daughter of an industrialist, as well) is metaphorically raped by a black man—sexism, classism, racism, and aesthetic hierarchies converge.

But, given its historical context, should the novel's consistently reactionary politics surprise us? Perhaps not. But what *is* surprising is that the figuration of women and African Americans is rarely mentioned in the scholarship. When it is, such figuration is routinely excused or cleverly and ultimately unpersuasively recontextualized. As the cultural critic Jan Nederveen Pieterse asks, "[W]hat interests of whites [or more specifically white males] are being served by these representations?"[4] In other words, we are grappling with interpretive biases similar to those that I have remarked upon in the criticism of *The Great Gatsby*. John Callahan's seminal *Illusions of a Nation*, for example, boldly breaking with prior approaches to Fitzgerald's work, foregrounds his sociological and historical meanings as opposed to the by-then-tedious details of his life and career. Although today we could comfortably label Callahan a new historicist, what remains troubling about his argument is the clear interest in proclaiming Fitzgerald a progressive, with the result that the valorization, when it occurs, of white bourgeois conventions and desires is either minimized or dismissed as parody. And yet Callahan's study informs what follows because, although its conclusions are radically different, it concerns itself with the same sociological issues.

Fitzgerald, argues André Le Vot, "reinvent[ed]" James's American "girl," "put her across as a model for his contemporaries, . . . show[ed] her no longer as a victim, but as victorious, as bold as the Daisy Millers of the past, but successful, independent, invulnerable."[5] It is certainly true that Fitzgerald is keenly aware of the Jamesian legacy. But as I have argued of *The Great Gatsby*, James's female archetypes are, in Fitzgerald's work, unrecoverable: sustained belief in America as female nurturer, as salvatory virgin, is no longer possible. And *Tender Is the Night* articulates the same frustration. Finally, Fitzgerald's women—flappers who do not become philosophers—are the emblems of loss.

Rosemary, whose point of view organizes book one, is initially equated with innocence, and indeed, calling up the conventions of the classic international tale, with America itself: "Her eyes were bright, big, clear, wet, and shining, the color of her cheeks was real, breaking close to the surface from the strong young pump of her heart. Her body hovered delicately on the last edge of childhood—she was almost eighteen, nearly complete, but the dew was still on her" (10). But female innocence in *Tender Is the Night* is merely a reproduction. Though in some senses the novel falls within the Jamesian tradition of female *Bildung*, taking its inexperienced heroine from the "littoral" into the interior (and consequently exposing her to the ways of the world), it quickly becomes clear that Rosemary is at a complete remove from the Master's Isabel or even his Daisy. The color of her cheeks may be "real," but it is also a commodity she freely exploits in order to advance her film career. To the extent that Rosemary is a function of, rather than a solution to, the cultural dilemma as Fitzgerald conceives it, her career in cinema can be seen as symptomatic of the forces contributing to the "decline of the West."[6]

Although in *The Crack-Up* Fitzgerald denies film the status of art, *Tender Is the Night* reads like a movie script. As Callahan argues, "we see the social world as a moving stage, its characters as a cast of actors and a director (Diver). It's as if a camera with a far-sighted lens sweeps over the Riviera disclosing nature and the evolving, dissolving human scene. . . ."[7] If film has no place in Fitzgerald's ideal America, its conventions nevertheless provide the structure for the story he has to tell. About to enter "an old Gaumont lot in process of reconstruction," Rosemary, we are told, "might have been looking into Hollywood" (30). Courting a high-brow readership by paying homage to Keats's "Ode to a Nightingale" and by arranging time psychologically (which is to say in a vaguely Joycean fashion), *Tender Is the Night* also tips its hat to the masses, caters to the supposedly insatiable public curiosity about the production of movies. The careful reconstruction of Hollywood techniques and of Hollywood itself may point up Fitzgerald's fear that the American enthusiasm for film had already spread, like an incurable virus, to the Old World, but it also suggests that he too had succumbed—like so many of his contemporaries—to the "grosser power" of movies of which he writes in *The Crack-Up*.[8]

Pondering whether an affair with Earl Brady, a director, will advance her career, Rosemary reflects: "If her person was property she could exercise whatever advantage was inherent in its ownership" (31). So the issue here is commodification. But Rosemary's willingness to trade her flesh for goods incurs both narrative scorn and praise. If in this text everyone is commodified (after all, Nicole's father essentially buys Dick, and Rosemary's mother peddles her daughter from producer to producer), then success depends on learning to choose one's markets wisely. Rosemary's education on the Riviera begins with a lesson in manners: the "far-reaching delicacy" of men like Abe North and Dick Diver, she comes to learn, is preferable to the "rough and ready good fellowship" (26) of actors and directors. Far better, then, to buy and sell at Villa Diana (the Diver compound) than in the studio, where "quick-lunch shack[s]" (30) and incessant talk of cost ("Baby, you don't take off the stockings, you can spoil ten more pairs. That dress is fifteen pounds" [31]) reveal that film is not art; it is systematic production. Insofar as it reifies the film world, *Tender Is the Night* brings labor into clear light, and yet at the same time it warns against the interpenetration of the classes. The sense of urgency brought to the representation of film implies an interest in reclaiming the old novel of manners, in which labor was seldom acknowledged in any sustained way, but in appropriating this genre Fitzgerald is unable to avoid breaking what presumably was once a sturdy frame.

As the potential heroine of a text committed to the genteel status quo but compelled to admit realities lurking beyond the drawing room door, Rosemary ascends from the "middle of the middle class" (63) to the pinnacle of bourgeois privilege. In this, she threatens the textual authority of Nicole, to whom she is constantly compared, because inherited money and pedigree are no longer the prerequisites, in this reconstructed world, for either social or textual legitimacy.

Playing the ingenue in a film entitled *Daddy's Girl*, a sentimental extravaganza designed to make women "forget the dirty dishes at home and weep" (80), Rosemary projects innocence with consummate skill: "there she was—*so* young and innocent—the product of her mother's loving care; there she was—embodying all the immaturity of the race, cutting a new cardboard paper doll to pass before its empty harlot's mind" (80). But this filmic virtue, as false as the frontier mother's croon, is incapable of redeeming a society absorbed in its own harlotry, which, we infer, film ultimately ex-

acerbates. More than this, *Daddy's Girl* anticipates another of the
novel's major motifs: incest. When Dick sees the film, he is particularly struck by its closing sequence, in which "Rosemary and her
parent [are] united at the last in a father complex so apparent that
Dick winced for all psychologists at the vicious sentimentality"
(81).

Nicole Diver and her father, Devereux Warren, were lovers;
the relationship in fact drove her to insanity. Callahan attributes
Fitzgerald's explicit indictment of films like *Daddy's Girl* to their
ability to seduce "a nation away from psychological and historical
realities . . . into a territory of illusions where order and sanity are
achieved, *finally*, by the happy ending."[9] And yet *Tender Is the Night*
ultimately endorses Hollywood's narrative strategies. For the
neurasthenic Nicole does achieve sanity, does find herself the
comparative victor in a novel that on "B-picture" terms resolves
itself happily. Because film governs her responses to experience,
Callahan finds Rosemary contemptible. "In short," he argues, "she
does not understand her movie's relation to the world. Even if she
knew Nicole's mystery, she would not be able to see that she, as
heroine of *Daddy's Girl*, came to fame by participation in a horrifying euphemistic fantasy of the Warren incest."[10] Again, this reading assumes that *Tender Is the Night* distinguishes itself from com-
mercial film. But Rosemary, arguably, is a Hollywood type: the
corruptible good girl helplessly drawn to "bad company." And
Nicole is a bad girl who, were it not for her money, would be
good.

Indeed, Nicole's literal investment in the capitalist system is
her art, and capitalism, is becomes clear, not only permits her
incestuous relationship with her father but precipitates it. Warren,
"a fine American type in every way, tall, broad, well-made" (143),
shares the same physical massiveness that Nick sees in Tom Buchanan, who "seemed to fill . . . [his] boots until he strained the
top lacing, and you could see a great pack of muscle shifting when
his shoulder moved under his thin coat. It was a body capable of

enormous leverage—a cruel body" (7). By bringing his adolescent daughter to his bed, Warren too has been cruel with his body, but the novel is less concerned with the taboo than with getting us to see that Nicole, like Rosemary, is herself a commodity. On these terms, what is truly "degenerate" (147), to invoke Warren's description of his own behavior, is capitalism itself.

The undeniable contempt in *Tender Is the Night* for the commodification of human relationships masks the novel's nostalgia for traditional gender roles. The real devastation in the text is not incest as such, conceived as economic exchange; rather, it is Nicole's immasculation. In her intimacy with Warren, she is truly Daddy's girl, which is to say Daddy's double. Her archetypal beauty notwithstanding, Nicole is identified with conventional masculine responsibilities, indeed, with masculinity itself. Not only does she designate her husband chief housekeeper and nurse ("for the purpose of . . . [Nicole's] cure, . . . [Dick] had for many years pretended to a rigid domesticity" [192]) but she also eschews the role of mother: "Dick, bringing up children [Nicole] could only pretend gently to love, guided orphans" (203).

Domesticated, obliged to mother, Dick is in essence a woman, and Nicole, in effect, is a man, doling out funds, retaining full control of her income and keeping her husband: "wanting to own him, . . . [she] encouraged any slackness on . . . [Dick's] part, and in multiplying ways he was constantly inundated by a trickling of goods and money" (192). Nicole's exponentially increasing wealth further disempowers a man who, on the Riviera, wears "transparent black lace drawers" (29), whose total emasculation, in short, is associated with the ultimate threat to culture (assuming that culture—namely, white bourgeois culture—depends on repetition, on reproduction): homosexuality. Nicole's buying power is the equivalent of her father's physical power; it, too, is manly:

Nicole bought from a great list that ran two pages, and bought the things in the windows besides. Everything she liked that she couldn't possibly use herself, she bought as a present for a friend. She bought colored beads, folding beach cushions, artificial flowers, honey, a guest bed, bags, scarfs, love birds, miniatures for a doll's house and three yards of some new cloth the color of prawns. She bought a dozen bathing suits, a rubber alligator, a travelling chess set of gold and ivory, big linen handkerchiefs for Abe, two chamois leather jackets of kingfisher blue and burning bush from Hermes. (65)

But if as a capitalist Nicole "contain[s] in herself her own doom" (65), in mass-market terms the text ultimately accords her a qualified success: she regains full control of her psyche and marries a second time. However, just as *Tender Is the Night* cloaks its political conservatism in the language of radicalism, so it conceals its attack on female empowerment in a plot structure in which women only appear to emerge victorious, when in fact they are disciplined and punished. In the end, Nicole may be rich and emotionally stable, but we can reasonably predict that she will continue to devour the men in her life. In short, because she is her own man, she is destined to be manless. Her economic and psychological triumph, then, is achieved by sacrificing Dick, who—in Fitzgeraldian terms—returns to America hardly a man at all: broken, confined to a deeper exile than he knew in Europe.

The luxurious isolation of Villa Diana, made possible by Nicole's money, appears to Rosemary as cohesiveness. In her eyes Dick and Nicole have achieved the familial solidarity that Nick Carraway finds so painfully absent in West Egg. Rosemary observes that on the Riviera Dick is "all complete" (27) and that the members of his summer entourage "obviously formed a self-sufficient little group" (23). But the harmony of their reinvented America is a lie. Villa Diana is literally a small city on a hill; and, like John Winthrop's New Israelite citadel, it is under siege. The threat to the Diver compound inserts itself quietly, almost humorously. Relying on the topos of America as garden, *Tender Is the*

Night emphasizes the destruction necessary to clear a space for Nicole's flower borders and vegetable beds, and at the same time it points at the parasites positioning themselves for attack. Of Nicole's obsession with cultivation, Dick says: "Nicole's garden. . . . She won't let it alone—she nags it all the time, worries about its diseases. Any day now I expect to have her come down with Powdery Mildew or Fly Speck, or Late Blight" (37). But aphids and beetles are not the only unwelcome visitors at Villa Diana. There is also the fungus of blackness.

In the early chapters of book one, race is submerged. The social conflicts besetting Villa Diana appear, on the whole, to relate to the violation of boundaries of class and art—until one reexamines the initially puzzling reference to Harriet Beecher Stowe. Dick's son and daughter are, respectively, Lanier and Topsy. The boy's name calls up the poetry of Sidney Lanier (a Southerner and, on the evidence of his work, an apologist for slavery, whose presence at this point in the text anticipates Dick's valorization of the Confederacy), his sister's the archetypal slave "girl" in *Uncle Tom's Cabin*. Stowe's Topsy is a clown, a minstrel, who, before Evangeline converts her (cajoles her, that is, into becoming a Christian obedient), wreaks havoc on the St. Claire household. Little Eva convinces a slave that in God's kingdom all are welcome: "[God] will help you to be good; and you can go to Heaven at last, and be an angel forever, just as much as if you were white. . . ."[11] Of this conversion, Jane Tompkins writes that "by giving Topsy her love, Eva initiates a process of redemption whose power, transmitted from heart to heart, can change the entire world."[12] And yet Stowe equates whiteness with beauty, virtue, and salvation; and blackness with ugliness, depravity, and damnation—an intractable associative pattern in *Tender Is the Night* as well.

Topsy is assured of God's boundless love, of the Christian extended family. Chanting "Au Clair de la Lune," the Diver children pray for admission into the Holy City: "Ouvre-moi ta porte / Pour l'amour de Dieu" (37). Whether heaven's door will open, however, is questionable. A potential filiative union between a white Southerner and a slave is, in this context, a veritable horror. The "true goal of Stowe's rhetorical undertaking," argues Tompkins, "is nothing less than the institution of the kingdom of heaven on earth."[13] At the end of her novel, however, Stowe solves the dilemma of slavery by advocating the return of Uncle Tom's people to Africa. Though *Tender Is the Night* may in fact mock Stowe's piety, it nevertheless evinces a persistent nostalgia for her position on the race problem. For the textual world that Lanier and Topsy inhabit privileges exclusion rather than community—in heaven or on earth.

The extent to which blacks, Afro-American and Afro-European, threaten the white exile's idea of order in France is central to the novel. When the narrative shifts from the Riviera to Paris, Dick and the principal actors of Villa Diana are immediately embroiled in a small "race riot" (112). Brief details of a plot that Fitzgerald must have considered exceedingly risqué are necessary. Abe North, who (so Dick, Nicole, and Rosemary assume) is on his way to America, decides against the trip and returns to Paris. At some point during his drunken pub crawl through Montmartre and Montparnasse he is robbed. He files a complaint, and the police dutifully arrest the criminal: "We have arrested a Negro," they inform an astonished Nicole. "We are convinced we have at last arrested the correct Negro" (110). The events that follow reduce to a few pages roughly two hundred years of Afro-American history, ultimately commenting on the novel's investment in inscribing racism.

Black exiles in *Tender Is the Night* are caricatures. Jules Peterson manufactures shoe polish—a clear reference to blackface. Though given the dubious distinction of being a "respectable Negro, on the suave model that heels the Republican party in the border States" (120), he behaves like Topsy: "his insincere eyes . . . roll-[ing] white semicircles of panic into view" (121–22). And Freeman, the personification both of emancipation and of the emergent nineteenth-century black bourgeoisie, is a "prominent Negro restaurateur" (121). The others are nameless—stock characters in a *corps de ménestrel*: "In brief, Abe had succeeded in the space of an hour in entangling himself with the personal lives, consciences, and emotions of one Afro-European and three Afro-Americans inhabiting the French Latin quarter" (121). As Michel Fabre argues in *La Rive Noire*, white American exiles of the 1920s and 1930s either did not know or chose to ignore that Langston Hughes, Claude McKay, and Jessie Fauset were their neighbors.[14] And *Tender Is the Night* is in this regard a comment in just such blindnesses. When blacks are the focus, the language deployed hybridizes the minstrel show with the kind of racist diatribe advanced, not surprisingly, in Griffith's *Birth of a Nation* or in Stoddard's *Rising Tide of Color*. Indeed, echoes of Tom Buchanan's conviction that the white race must defend itself are numerous.

While lunching at their hotel, the "trio" of Dick, Rosemary, and Nicole—having taken temporary refuge from the Civil War resurging around them—are drawn to and comforted by the *"families* [my emphasis] of Americans staring around at families of Americans" (114). But one group, a gathering of war widows, proves especially noteworthy: "[T]he party gave the impression of a unit. . . . Certainly it was more of a unit than any conceivable tourist party" (114). In these women Dick "perceive[s] all the maturity of an older America" (115): "Momentarily, he sat again on his father's knee, riding with Moseby [*sic;* John Singleton Mosby, a Confederate] while the old loyalties and devotions fought on around him" (115). Dick's identification with the Confederates can easily be dismissed as further indication of his romanticism and not of his politics. Edwin Fussell, for example, argues that Dick's reverie merely points up Fitzgerald's tendency to see "in the quest for romantic wonder a recurrent pattern of American behavior."[15]

The Confederates, after all, were rebels with a cause, rising against an oppressive federalism. And yet, since this memory seizes Dick in an atmosphere of considerable racial tension, its political implications cannot be ignored. Whether one views the Civil War as a territorial dispute or a battle over slavery (economics), it nevertheless resulted in the liberation of an entire race. Given that the Confederates resolved to destroy a political and metaphorical union, Dick's indifference to the "loyalties and devotions" of the North attests to his politics. Is the "older America" he invokes the antebellum South, and is Abe North the eponymous symbol of Yankee aggression who, by "entangling" himself with blacks, serves as a painful reminder of the racial consequences of the war? Callahan's reading of the Mosby reference is perceptive:

> "Old loyalties and devotions"? . . . These ideals mean one thing in the *legend* of chivalry and another in the *history* of America, particularly that of the South. Slavery and aristocracy; toil and leisure; white virgins worshipped, black women raped. In repetition of his personal fantasies and desires, Diver superimposes chivalric legend upon gruesome history.[16]

Callahan, however, is careful to distinguish Dick Diver's rhetoric from F. Scott Fitzgerald's. But this is not an easy task. Predictably, he sees the uproar of the Peterson episode as parody, as a parody of "black-white relations."[17] But assigning a radical politics to Fitzgerald necessitates revalorizing the very discursive oppositions that, as a critic whose work anticipates contemporary methodologies, Callahan presumably would abandon. If the self in a novel is a construction, so too is the self in, for example, a letter. I am suggesting that whether one chooses to examine Fitzgerald's fictions or his private, ostensibly nonfictional discourse, there are consistent and ultimately discomfiting ideologies that as a marginalized reader I find disturbing. Consider, for example, this fragment from a letter (May 1921) to Edmund Wilson:

God damn the continent of Europe. It is merely of antiquarian interest. Rome is only a few years behind Tyre and Babylon. The negroid streak creeps northward to defile the Nordic race. Already the Italians have the souls of blackamoors. Raise the bars of immigration and permit only Scandinavians, Teutons, Anglo-Saxons and Celts to enter. France made me sick. Its silly pose as the thing the world has to save. I think it's a shame that England and America didn't let Germany conquer Europe. It's the only thing that would have saved the fleet of tottering old wrecks. My reactions were all philistine, antisocialistic, provincial and racially snobbish. I believe at last in the white man's burden. We are as far above the modern Frenchman as he is above the Negro.[18]

Is this, as Callahan would have us read the Peterson episode, an ingenious parody of a bigoted consciousness? Possibly. The ability to accept such a letter as confirmation of Fitzgerald's sense of play or as evidence of his driving ambition to prove to Wilson that he was at bottom a tough-minded writer with a taste for the scatological and the incendiary ultimately depends on readerly politics. Since I am not a white liberal, it is difficult for me to resist calling a rhetorical spade a spade.

All this invites a deeper reading of the Peterson affair. Not only Dick but the novel itself is anxious to rescue Rosemary and Nicole from an "atmosphere of unfamiliar Negro faces bobbing up in unexpected places and around unexpected corners . . ." (121). Peterson's body somehow ends up in Rosemary's room. The explanation for Peterson's death, framed in the discourse of a frontier skirmish, is "that Abe's first hostile Indian had tracked the friendly Indian and discovered him in the corridor, and when the latter had taken desperate refuge in Rosemary's room, had hunted down and slain him" (125). Here the language compares with an earlier description of Peterson, who had verified Abe's story during the police interrogation, as a man "rather in the position of the friendly Indian who had helped a white" (121). Not only is the history of the early settlement of America written into the text but so is yet another suggestion of Stowe. Peterson, it becomes clear, is an Uncle Tom whose first loyalty is to the master as opposed to the slave. There is a strong implication that his betrayal and the dissension it engenders typify blacks. They are like stereotypical nineteenth-century American "Injuns": murderers, thieves, rapists.

Indeed, Rosemary's brief encounter with Peterson suggests a rape: "She opened the door of her room and went directly to her desk where she had suddenly remembered leaving her wristwatch. It was there; slipping it on she glanced down at the daily letter to her mother, finishing the last sentence in her mind. Then, rather gradually, she realized without turning about that she was not alone in the room . . . [;] a dead Negro was stretched upon her bed" (124). Rosemary, the white "virgin," escapes actual violation (by a black man, at any rate), but the images associated with rape are firmly planted in our minds. There is blood on the bedspread, and Dick observes that "there would be faint blood on the blanket beneath" (125). Recognizing that a movie star who plays the ingenue cannot be implicated in a situation "as remote from her as sickness" (122), Dick moves the body to the corridor, to (in effect) the textual margin, telling Rosemary: "Look here, you mustn't get upset over this—it's only some nigger scrap" (125).

But everyone is implicated in the "nigger scrap" that Dick is so desperate to flee. Indeed, the Peterson episode not only condenses much of the novel, it also occasions its central crises. It precipitates, for example, Nicole's mental relapse, an outburst so powerful that it "penetrate[s] the keyholes and the cracks in the doors, swe[eps] into [Rosemary's] suite and in the shape of horror t[akes] form again" (127). And thus it foreshadows the investigation of the Divers' emotionally explosive marriage—the focus of books two and three. And, further, for the residents of Dick's "community" of exiles, it clears away any possibility of imagining France a refuge from America. This is not, as Malcolm Cowley would have us believe, simply "a psychological novel about the glory and decline of Richard Diver."[19] It is, instead, a far more demanding text, one that forces us not only to hear the wolves lurking outside the cabin door, but to name them.

4

The Beast in
Giovanni's Room

Giovanni's Room is a well-known Philadelphia bookstore physically, and perhaps figuratively as well, at the center of the gay community. It takes its name, of course, from the novel Baldwin published in 1956, the book about which nobody is neutral and many, even now, are frankly indignant. As Henry Louis Gates, Jr., has recently suggested, "*Giovanni's Room*, arguably Baldwin's most accomplished novel, is seldom taught in black literature classes because its characters are white *and* gay."[1] In the neoconservative era of Allan Bloom, E. D. Hirsch, Dinesh D'Souza, Camille Paglia, the implications of Baldwin's homosexual thematics, for whites and for blacks, may be as unsettling today as they were nearly thirty years ago, when Robert Bone argued that "to most, homosexuality will seem an evasion rather than an affirmation of human truth."[2]

Conceived as a resource center for a community with few resources, the bookstore in question is itself a structure of interpretation. For its custodians imply not only that one *can* take refuge there but that doing so is imperative. Which is a troubling position on the eponymous text, if indeed we can assume that Baldwin finally makes it clear that living in what is in effect a closet is an absurdity. Like the bookstore, gay critical inquiry is a thing apart, teeters on the academic margin. Indeed, there is a decided resistance among mainstream readers of Henry James to engage the complexities of sexual desire in his work—out of the fear, as Eve Sedgwick maintains in *Epistemology of the Closet,*[3] of sullying his reputation, of transforming him into a marginal figure. Though critics frequently cower in the face of a possible Jamesian homopoetics, Baldwin *as novelist* does not. It will become clear that *Giovanni's Room* revises "The Beast in the Jungle," naming what the Master will not name, chaining the figure of the beast to the taboo of homosexuality.

In a somewhat problematic reading of Baldwin's still controversial novel, Claude Summers argues that its "artistic vision . . . necessitated a white American as protagonist."[4] Why? Certainly, it is acutely aware of the Jamesian international tale, subsuming as it does the angst, the dispossession undergirding James's portraits of Americans abroad. And yet the suggestion that blackness has been erased is misleading. Although the narrator is white, as is every other figure in the text, racial oppression is an implicit concern. Consider Baldwin's dramatic beginning:

> I stand at the window of this great house in the south of France as night falls, the night which is leading me to the most terrible morning of my life. I have a drink in my hand, there is a bottle at my elbow. I watch my reflection in the darkening gleam of the window pane. My reflection is tall, perhaps rather like an arrow, my blond hair gleams. My face is like a face you have seen many times. My ancestors conquered a continent, pushing across death-laden plains, until they came to an ocean which faced away from Europe into a darker past.[5]

This startles for several reasons. When *Giovanni's Room* first appeared, Baldwin already enjoyed a reputation as one of the pre-

mier African-American writers of his day. Anointed by the white
establishment, after the publication of *Go Tell It on the Mountain*, as
the new spokesperson for the black community, he wrote a second book that, ostensibly, had nothing to do with blackness—
that challenged the institutionally embedded idea that the scope
of black writing was narrow. And so on one level *Giovanni's Room*
is virtuoso nose thumbing. Still, given his unrelenting commitment to achieving parity for blacks, Baldwin's decision to organize
the text around a white consciousness was more than a calculated
rebuff or a clever joke. For David acknowledges his complicity in
racial conquest. And his recognition marks the beginning of an
associative pattern compelling the reader to explore the connec-
tions linking Giovanni's persecution with the African American's.
For we are never permitted to forget that David's convoluted,
often self-delusional musings are the invention of a black man.

Summers points out that *Giovanni's Room* is central to the gay
canon. And it undoubtedly is. Yet it is not simply the story of a
young man's emergence from the closet. Though I am about to
argue that it rewrites, indeed, homoeroticizes James, it also lays
claim to the legacy of Richard Wright. Critics have frequently
remarked upon Baldwin's complicated relationship with the writer
he called his "spiritual father,"[6] expatiating upon the critical salvos
of "Everybody's Protest Novel" and "Alas, Poor Richard." Eldridge
Cleaver, for example, argues in *Soul on Ice* that the latter "essay . . .
reveals that he despised—not Richard Wright—but his masculinity."[7] This is Cleaver at his homophobic best. Still, the gap between Wright and Baldwin may not be so wide. For *Giovanni's
Room*, oddly omitted from Cleaver's discussion, falls within the
very tradition of protest from which Baldwin supposedly sought
to distance himself. In his introduction to *Native Son*, Wright dis-
cusses his dissatisfaction with earlier work, calling *Uncle Tom's Children* "a book which even bankers' daughters could read and weep
over and feel good about. I swore to myself that if I ever wrote
another book, no one would weep over it; that it would be so

hard and deep that they would have to face it without the conso-
lation of tears."[8] Baldwin's novel abhors sentimentality as well,
slapping the face of middle-class white America, chipping away
at its preoccupations and blindnesses with each new page. It is
in some senses, as Horace Porter has explained, a reconstructed
Native Son.[9]

There can be little doubt that the revelations of a homosexual
narrator would have been as shocking to Baldwin's readers as Bigger's uncompromising violence was to Wright's. Since in both
narratives the taboo is a weapon aimed at the establishment,
Cleaver's dismissal of Baldwin as a writer whose "work is . . . void
of a political, economic, or even a social reference" is a distortion,[10] and yet beneath the vitriol lies a sincere concern about the
dimensions of Baldwin's political design. Was he a monoculturalist who yearned for an indissoluble union between blacks and
whites? If he can be categorized at all, then Baldwin is best understood as a biculturalist who was unwilling to ignore the role white
culture had played in defining a new and possibly uniquely American blackness. Since in his work the reluctance to challenge
white patriarchal icons like James is so pronounced, he at times
seems a perverse conservative, and this conservatism runs
throughout his writing on race *and* homosexuality. In the end *Giovanni's Room* is less a critique of Jamesian homosexual repression
than an apology for it.

If in our hunger for political and sexual outlaws we turn to
Baldwin, only to find him lacking on both counts, then we are
perhaps overlooking the subtle power of his work, which depends
upon the ability to confront the establishment on its own terms.
Fully conversant with hegemonic discursive maneuvers, Baldwin
counterattacks with a response that only looks like a concession
to white authority. His roots, in short, lie in the African-American
tradition of performance, in which the audience (the readership)—together with its reflexes and orientations—becomes the
endlessly acted-upon, although unwitting, subject. As novelist or

essayist, Baldwin is therefore difficult to pin down—to such a degree that David Bergman (*Gaiety Transfigured*) mistakes his reticence on homosexuality for "discomfort with the subject,"[11] when it may be instead a refusal to be marginalized and thus neutralized. Baldwin's strategy, a strategy for professional survival and for a degree of political control in a culture hostile to black dissent, cannot be dehistoricized, despite the fact that we may wince today at its conciliatory veneer.

Like *The Great Gatsby*, *Giovanni's Room* is an extended confession, its classic unreliable narrator wholly unattuned to his own biases. To begin with, David is a homophobe. The effeminate Guillaume, for example, whom Giovanni strangles, is rendered so repellent as to be of another species: "[H]is utter grotesqueness made me uneasy; perhaps in the same way that the sight of monkeys eating their own excrement turns some people's stomachs. They might not mind so much if monkeys did not—so grotesquely—resemble human beings" (40). The narration moves swiftly from bestiality to cannibalism. On his way to Giovanni's room for the first time, David remarks that "a butcher had already opened his shop and one could see him within, already bloody, hacking at the meat" (64). Les Halles, the market district (David is obsessed with the economics of sex), is a desert of decay: "The pavements were slick with leavings, mainly cast-off, rotten leaves, flowers, fruit, and vegetables which had met with disaster natural and slow, or abrupt. And the walls and corners were combed with *pissoirs*, make-shift cafés, restaurants, and smokey yellow bistros . . ." (70). This, clearly, is hell. But, cast in the role of representative white bourgeois male, David does not invoke Dante, or even Eliot. Instead, he turns to the horror picture for the images he needs both to convey his own terror and, of course, to scare "us" to death. The homosexual prototype is a thing risen from the dead: "It looked like a mummy or a zombie. . . . And it walked, really, like someone who might be sleepwalking or like those figures in slow motion one sometimes sees on the screen. It carried a glass, it

walked on its toes, the flat hips moved with a dead, horrifying
lasciviousness" (57). Predatory ghoul, the homosexual male is sure
to get you.

David is unable to envision living as a homosexual without
duplicating or parodying heterosexual practices and conventions.
And yet this capitulation to heterosexual authority is not, within
Baldwin's textual world at any rate, unusual. *Another Country*, for
example, as I shall point out in Chapter 7, presents gay characters
who are similarly frustrated. Explaining why his "relationship"
with Giovanni can never be, David offers this gendered rational-
ization to the lover he so desperately wants both to escape and
to possess: "You want to go out and be the big laborer and bring
home the money and you want me to stay here and wash the
dishes and cook the food and clean this miserable closet of a
room and kiss you when you come in through that door and lie
with you at night and be your little *girl*" (208). But Giovanni does
not want a parody of a woman; he wants a man. Guillaume's bar,
the repressive emblem of the gay subculture (it is an "ill-lit sort of
tunnel" [38]), is popular with *"les folles,* [who] always dressed in
the most improbable combinations, screaming like parrots the details of their latest love-affairs. . . . Occasionally one would swoop
in . . . to convey the news that he—but they always called each
other 'she'—had just spent time with a celebrated movie star, or
boxer" (39). David—"Butch" (131), as his father calls him—insists
that he is not a woman, and he is equally adamant about the
sexual illegitimacy of these effeminate men: "I always found it
difficult to believe that they ever went to bed with anybody for a
man who wanted a woman would certainly not want one of *them*"
(39). But if David yearns for a world in which men are always
manly and women irrefutably feminine, then it is worth mentioning that his female lovers are defiantly masculine. Hella, his fian-
cée, is "wide-legged, boyish" (175). Sue, the woman he cruelly
seduces in an effort to reaffirm his masculinity, wears "her curly
blonde hair cut very short" (139), possesses "small breasts" (139),

and "almost always w[ears] tight blue jeans" (139). Though he reproves men who look and behave like women, he never acknowledges his own preference for women who look and behave like men.

As Jennie Livingston reveals in the remarkable *Paris Is Burning* (1991), there are many forms of drag, and David's obsessively manly pose is among them. Historicizing permutations within the gay subculture of cross-dressers and transsexuals, Livingston's film focuses on competitive balls, pageants really, in which African-American and Latino men in drag demonstrate that they have mastered white culture. Costumes are meticulously copied from the advertising pages of *Vogue, Harper's Bazaar, Gentlemen's Quarterly*. The contestants attempt to convince the judges (and the often hostile audience) that they are for the moment high-fashion models, schoolgirls, socialites—or, conversely, virile military officers, football players, manly corporate executives. The ultimate objective: to achieve what is called "realness." The film adroitly concludes that being a woman or a man, which is to say looking like one, is culturally determined. Obviously David, middle-American essentialist, responds only to sex and does not meditate on the complexities of gender. Livingston further suggests, as does Baldwin, that the oppression of homosexuals and the victimization of African Americans are not easily distinguishable. None of the young men in the film could be said to be privileged—in the socioeconomic sense. Their need to reproduce the opulence of the fashion pages comments on their disenfranchisement, for only at the balls are they able to sustain the illusion of self-worth, of personal achievement. I have suggested that in *Giovanni's Room* the male homosexual is both "real" and metaphorical. For the young men who come under David's wholly unsympathetic gaze are confined to a seemingly inescapable ghetto, are as marginalized as the African Americans Baldwin portrays in his first novel, *Go Tell It on the Mountain*.

A homosexual who despises homosexuals, David advances a

view of gay life that is as contemptuous of it as is Cleaver's. But David is also a misogynist. Acutely conscious of 1950s' ideology, the novel represents the cliché that men—whether repressed or sexually self-aware—who want men despise women. David's sexual "problems," predictably, can be traced back to early childhood. "My mother," he tells us, "had been carried to the graveyard when I was five. I scarcely remember her at all, yet she figured in my nightmares, blind with worms, her hair as dry as metal and brittle as a twig, straining to press me against her body; that body so putrescent, so sickening soft, that it opened, as I clawed and cried, into a breach so enormous as to swallow me alive" (15). This parodic Freudian moment is one more example of how Baldwin—as opposed to David—acknowledges the facile, although at the time generally accepted, theory that homosexuals either loved their mothers too much or, in their inability to become their mothers, grew to loathe them and consequently all women. David's dilemma, it would seem, is the latter. His father's sister Ellen, for example, is "over made-up, with a face and figure beginning to harden, and with too much jewelry everywhere, clanging and banging in the light" (16). Sue looks like a "broken down movie queen facing the cruel cameras again after a long eclipse" (145). And Hella, woman as demon, embodies a castratory power: "I was fantastically intimidated by her breasts, and when I entered her I began to feel that I would never get out alive" (232).

The novel struggles to get us to see both the inadequacy of Freudian homosexual theory and the brainwashing power of American bourgeois morality. For Giovanni's prenarrative history does not differ radically from David's, with the all-important exception—a mythology, a Jamesian romanticism—that he is Italian and is thus less repressed. In Italy Giovanni had once led an orthodox life, had loved and lived with a woman, had fathered a child, a child who died at birth. Giovanni understands this death as signal, destroying as it did his ability to believe in the religious and social traditions of his community: "When I knew that . . .

[the baby] was dead I took our crucifix off the wall and I spat on it and I threw it on the floor and my mother and my girl screamed and I went out" (205). Having buried the child in the "churchyard where . . . [his] father and . . . [his] father's fathers were" (204), he abandoned his village forever.

Although Giovanni regards his life in Paris, his life as a comparatively healthy homosexual among homosexual homophobes, as punishment for sins perpetrated against the Holy Father ("and then I left my village and I came to this city where surely God has punished me for all my sins and for spitting on His Holy Son, and where I will surely die" [205]), Baldwin undermines this view. What Giovanni does not realize, and what we are meant to, is that he has successfully thrown off the yoke of convention, has buried the metaphorical child in the churchyard, and has moved on. Although we may want to read the death of his son as confirmation that who he is and what he does goes against nature, *Giovanni's Room* ultimately decenters filiative bonds. The relationship that he envisions with David, in short, is or should be legitimate, but what stands in its way is culture itself.

Hence the wonderful figure of the room, the room Giovanni "had always had great plans for remodelling" (124). But neither he, David, nor finally Baldwin has a blueprint for the new world the novel envisions but cannot achieve. Giovanni's impulse is to tear the wallpaper down, to strip the place free of history and to start again. The wall opposite the one on which this cultural work has begun, however, "was destined never to be uncovered and on this wall a lady in a hoop skirt and a man in knee breeches perpetually walked together, hemmed in by roses" (124). Removing the impress of heterosexual authority, in other words, is not easy. Later, Giovanni attempts to demolish the wall—or at least to break through it: "He had some weird idea that it would be nice to have a bookcase sunk in the wall and he chipped through the wall until he came to the brick and began pounding away at the brick. It was hard work, it was insane work . . ." (167).

David's dismissal of this activity as "weird" and "insane" is consistent with his other biases, as is his refusal to participate: he cannot imagine remaining in the room under any circumstances. Indeed, in his most conventional moments, he longs to return to the dominant community, "to be inside again, with the light and safety, with my manhood unquestioned, watching my woman put my children to bed" (152). But does Baldwin share these desires? Does he, too, regard the room as a prison? In the novel's conclusion, which I shall discuss in greater detail later, David escapes all enclosures—Guillaume's underground bar, the room, the house rented with Hella—and walks in the open air, alone, though with some vague awareness of others. Have gay theorists and gay activists romanticized Baldwin's novel? We could say that Giovanni has at least a room of his own, but the oppressive presence of the heterosexual couple "hemmed in by roses" would seem to indicate that this is not the case.

When the *Village Voice* interviewed Baldwin in 1984, he insisted that *Giovanni's Room* "is not really about homosexuality. It's the vehicle through which the book moves. . . . It's about what happens to you if you're afraid to love anybody. Which is much more interesting than the question of homosexuality."[12] Naively universalist and somewhat coy, this is not a statement easily digested in the 1990s. Contemporary readers may also find Baldwin's acute sense of alienation within the gay community something of a surprise: "The word gay has always rubbed me the wrong way. I never understood exactly what is meant by it. . . . Even in my early years in the Village, what I saw of that world absolutely frightened me, bewildered me. I didn't understand the necessity of all the role playing. And in a way I still don't" (13). And: "You know, it never occurred to me to join a club. I must say I felt very much alone. But I was alone on so many levels and this was one more aspect of it" (13).

Although *Giovanni's Room* undertakes a kind of sexual liberation for its protagonist, it appears to endorse the very individualism, the aloneness, that Baldwin articulates in the *Voice* interview. But how does one survive without a community? When the interviewer put the question to him, Baldwin was evasive, arguing that "one's sexual preference is a private matter" (14) and that institutions are wrong to interfere with it. "But," he says, "it has been made a public question by the institutions of the country" (14). These remarks begin to take on all the complexity (and, indeed, all the ambiguity) of his second novel, for Baldwin admits that "if the so-called gay movement can cause men and women, boys and girls, to come to some kind of terms with themselves more speedily and with less pain, then that's a very great advance" (14). Presumably such a coming to terms would involve sweeping institutional reform, but to the suggestion that going one's own way in a hostile climate is perhaps self-destructive, Baldwin replies: "One has to make that climate for oneself" (15).

David's ideological stranglehold aside for the moment, it remains to be seen how *Giovanni's Room* helps us tease out Baldwin's reading of "The Beast in the Jungle" in particular and of James, potentially, in general. If the story is a study of psychosexual paralysis, then how seriously should we entertain the possibility of John Marcher's repressed homosexuality? On the evidence of *Giovanni's Room* alone, Baldwin saw homosexuality as a legitimate, if risky, subject for narrative. Curiously however, he never publicly discussed the issue of homosexual desire in James. Perhaps even Baldwin feared the consequences of openly associating the Master with so dangerous an idea. To the extent that Baldwin protected James, he accorded him the same protection he wanted for himself. What could not be said in an essay, however, could be broached (buried) in a novel. In part two of *Giovanni's Room* David expresses his deepest anxiety about homosexuality: "The beast which Giovanni had awakened in me would never sleep again; but one day I would not be with Giovanni anymore. And I would then, like all the others, find myself turning and following all kinds of boys down God knows what dark avenues, into what dark places? With this fearful intimation there opened in me a hatred for Giovanni which was as powerful as my love and which was nourished by the same roots" (122). As I will demonstrate, this is not the only point at which James's "beast" pushes through, but, arguably, it is the most telling. David understands homosexual behavior as irredeemably and uncontrollably promiscuous. That, in his view, is the nature of the beast.

Though it is true that Marcher is incapable of stating the issue so frankly (indeed, he never acknowledges the possibility of his homosexuality), the point is clear: Marcher, like David, is in a state of homosexual panic. In rewriting the tale, Baldwin attempts what James presumably was unable even to imagine: David's (Marcher's) sexual liberation. And at the same time he points up the risk one takes in challenging the sexual status quo. In the novel's final and ambiguous moments, when Giovanni is guillotined, David is all at once victim, executioner, narcissist, penitent, and lover:

> I walk into the bedroom where the clothes I will wear are lying on the bed and my bag lies open and ready. I begin to undress. There is a mirror in this room, a large mirror. I am terribly aware of the mirror. Giovanni's face swings before me like an unexpected lantern on a dark, dark night. . . . I see it in this mirror, out of the corner of my eye. . . . He kisses the cross and clings to it. The priest gently lifts the cross away. Then they lift Giovanni. The journey begins. They move off, toward another door. . . . That door is the gateway he has sought so long out of this dirty world, this dirty body. (245–47)

Stripping down before the mirror, anticipating his own reflection, David instead confronts the reflection of another and is unable to conceive of a way of reconciling his idea of himself with the image before him: "The body in the mirror forces me to turn and face it. And I look at my body, which is under sentence of death.

It is lean, hard, and cold, the incarnation of a mystery. And I do not know what moves in this body, what this body is searching. It is trapped in my mirror as it is trapped in time and it hurries toward revelation" (247). If by visualizing Giovanni's death David acknowledges his own complicity in the matter, he has yet to realize the extent to which an ultimately puritanical ideology has prevented him from achieving full selfhood. In other words, how does one construct a homosexual identity? Indeed, as will become clear, Baldwin returns to the figure of the mirror in *Another Country*, once again suggesting that the image of homosexuality is controlled and conditioned by others.

Guilt-ridden, David assigns Giovanni the role of Christ figure, denying the authority of Giovanni's "dirty body." And yet at the same time this is a sexual moment, one in which the naked David is acutely conscious of his genitals and, by implication, of Giovanni's. "I long to crack that mirror," he says, "and be free. I look at my sex, my troubling sex, and wonder how it can be redeemed, how I can save it from the knife. The journey to the grave is already begun, the journey to corruption is, always, already, half over. Yet the key to my salvation, which cannot save my body, is hidden in my flesh" (247).

When Giovanni literally loses his head, David contemplates losing his penis. Within the cultural scheme of things, Baldwin boldly suggests, homosexuals are either decapitated (sentenced to death for acting upon their desires) or metaphorically castrated because, fearing social death, they cannot act upon their desires. *Giovanni's Room* ends, not with the implication that David's life is over, as is Marcher's, but with the strong suggestion that it is just beginning. Homosexuality need not be the social death sentence that, throughout most of the narrative, David believes it to be:

> And at last I step out into the morning. . . . And I look up the road, where a few people stand, men and women, waiting for the morning bus. They are vivid beneath the awakening sky, and the

horizon beyond them is beginning to flame. The morning weighs on my shoulders with the dreadful weight of hope. . . . Yet, as I turn and begin walking toward the waiting people, the wind blows some of them back on me. (248)

Quite different from James's ending of doom:

He saw the Jungle of his life and saw the lurking Beast; then, while he looked, perceived it, as by a stir of the air, rise, huge and hideous, for the leap that was to settle him. His eyes darkened—it was close; and, instinctively turning, in his hallucination, to avoid it, he flung himself, face down, on the tomb.[13]

Though David may have a chance, in this reading (which is to say Baldwin's) his anxieties reproduce Marcher's. While living with Giovanni he is obsessed with being "found **out**" (118), desperately worried about Hella's uncovering the secret: "It's just that she'll be terribly hurt if she does find out, that's all. People have very dirty words for—for this situation. . . . Besides, it *is* a crime—in my country and, after all, I didn't grow up here, I grew up *there*" (118). Marcher too has something to hide, although we can never be entirely sure what it is: "It had never entered into his plan that any one should 'know,' and mainly for the reason that it wasn't in him to tell any one. . . . He had thought himself, so long as nobody knew, the most disinterested person in the world, carrying his concentrated burden, his perpetual suspense, ever so quietly, holding his tongue about it, giving others no glimpse of it nor of its effect upon this life . . ." (495–96). We also know that "he had a screw loose for . . . [Bartram], but she liked him in spite of it. . . . The rest of the world thought him queer, but she, she only, knew how, and above all why queer . . ." (498–99). And we know that Bartram "traced his unhappy perversion through reaches of its course into which he could scarce follow it" (499).

If by this point Eve Sedgwick's importance for my work is obvious, I do have some reservations about her overall endeavor. Though possibly no one has done as much for gay theory as she has, one begins to wonder whether she intends to rescue the literary homosexual from the closet or to excoriate men for what they have done to women. As she writes in *Between Men*, "in any male-dominated society, there is a special relationship between male homosocial (*including* homosexual) desire and the structures for maintaining and transmitting patriarchal power."[14] And so, though her study announces itself as a much needed investigation of "men's relations with other men" (2), it turns out to be an intricate analysis of female invisibility within the range of texts she scrutinizes. In the more recent *Epistemology of the Closet*, Sedgwick states her agenda plainly. Her reading of "The Beast in the Jungle," for example, ends up reproving Marcher, in surprisingly conventional ways, for his failure to see who May Bartram "really" is. In Sedgwick's view Marcher victimizes Bartram, sentencing her to "imprisonment in . . . [his] closet—an imprisonment that, the story makes explicit, is founded on his inability to perceive or value her as a person beyond her complicity in his view of his predicament."[15]

Well, yes, but how do we account for Sedgwick's thinly veiled critical contempt for Marcher and, by implication, for James? What, in short, would she have either of them do? Apparently, she would like to see Bartram "rounded and whole," less "bracketed," so that we could be clear about *her* "emotional determinants" and about *her* "needs and desires" (199). What Marcher wants—or does not know he wants—is, in her reading, almost irrelevant. Announcing that she will speak "less equivocally from . . . [her] own eros and experience," Sedgwick sees Bartram as a woman who receives a certain "emotional" gratification from the company she keeps with a man in a state of (homosexual?) panic, even though, as Sedgwick observes, Marcher is an "otherwise boring" (209) man.

But how does the argument that, in Bartram, James offers a
portrait of a woman who not only prefers but seemingly is drawn
to a man who does not threaten her sexually make "The Beast in
the Jungle" "potentially revolutionary" (199)? Sedgwick "hypothe-
size[s] that what May Bartram would have liked for Marcher, the
narrative she wished to nurture for him, would have been a prog-
ress from a vexed and gaping self-ignorance around his homosexual possibilities to a self-knowledge of them that would have freed
him to find and enjoy a sexuality of whatever sort emerged" (207).
To suggest that Marcher ultimately controls Bartram is to assume
that whatever power he holds over her is a function of his maleness. Alternatively, I would argue that both figures are essentially
powerless and that they are collusive: they act out the role of man
and woman together, even though, obviously, neither is content
with it. Sedgwick implies that it is easier to be a sexually repressed
man than a sexually repressed woman. But surely neither condition is especially desirable. Nor, it would seem, does James in-
scribe a hierarchy of oppression in which Marcher emerges the
paradoxical victor.

I do not suggest that May Bartram's readiness to sacrifice herself, indeed, to die for Marcher, is of no critical interest; instead,
the life she lives, or rather does not live, comments on what the
culture expects of women, gives them to understand: namely, that
they are nothing and nowhere without men. (And, of course, a
man is nothing and nowhere without a woman.) What is evident
in "The Beast in the Jungle" is its frustration with the constraints
of gender. (And this frustration pervades Baldwin's revision of the
text.) May Bartram spends the bulk of the narrative waiting: waiting not only for Marcher to see her as the significant person she
unequivocally is, but also for some small measure of indepen-
dence. When her great-aunt dies, she inherits enough money to
run a house of her own. "She had," we are told, "acquired property" (494), and with it a degree of freedom she had never before

experienced. But Bartram's new ability to make a life for herself without deferring to others is, ideologically, not enough.

If Bartram sees herself (or is compelled to construe herself) as incomplete without a man, so Marcher is caught in the cultural trap of believing that he is incomplete without Bartram, without a woman:

> Above all she was in the secret of the difference between the forms he went through—those of his little office under Government, those of caring for his modest patrimony, for his library, for his garden in the country, for the people in London whose invitations he accepted and repaid—and the detachment that reigned beneath them and that made of all behaviour, all that could in the least be called behaviour, a long act of dissimulation. What it had come to was that he wore a mask painted with the social simper, out of the eyeholes of which there looked eyes of an expression not in the least matching the other features. This the stupid world, even after years, had never more than half-discovered. It was only May Bartram who had, and she achieved, by an art indescribable, the feat of at once—or perhaps it was only alternately—meeting the eyes from in front and mingling her own vision, as from over his shoulder, with their peep through the apertures. (499–500)

This is a slippery passage. Sedgwick understands it as proof that Marcher's "angle on daily existence and intercourse is that of the closeted person" (205). Perhaps—and yet the point of view is Bartram's: she, "meeting the eyes from in front and mingling her own vision," observes a man who to her is a study in self-deception, whose existence is meaningless—unless, that is, he agrees to share his life with her. Under different cultural circumstances, Bartram might have affirmed Marcher's possible pleasure in tending his garden alone—might have applauded, in short, his attempt to invent a domestic space for himself and by himself.

A socialized woman, Bartram defines herself in terms of ministering to men. So does Baldwin's Hella. Having spent several months in Spain living without a man, Hella returns to David urging him to marry her. Although marriage is what she says she wants, she considers it institutionalized estrangement: "[We] might get married now and stay married for fifty years and I might be a stranger to you every instant of that time and you might never know it. . . . For a woman, . . . I think a man is always a stranger. And there's something awful about being at the mercy of a stranger" (183). Nevertheless, having a man "to take care of and feed and torment and trick and love" (185) is in her view the only way for a woman to construct a self. Baldwin, I am suggesting, is sensitive to James's critique of wedlock, a critique reaching its apex with *The Golden Bowl*, which, as Joseph Boone argues, "implicates the hierarchy of male and female roles that too often transforms love relationship[s] into a battle for mastery and possession."[16] Boone reminds us that the novel is split in two; book one assumes the perspective of the Prince and book two that of the Princess, thus pointing up "the sexual division that separates husband and wife, locks them into antagonistic roles, and bars each access to the other's objective thoughts, feelings, and needs" (193–94). Like *The Golden Bowl*, *Giovanni's Room* also divides in half, simultaneously co-opting James's marital skepticism and calling for, though not achieving, new ways of conceiving relationships—whether between men and women or between men who, on the evidence of David and Giovanni, are stifled by heterosexual role models.

When David rejects Hella, she assumes he does so because *she* has failed him. Hella is an intellectual, but on learning that David no longer wants her she makes a desperate offer to transform herself into a conventional woman—submissive, unambiguously feminine: "David, please let me be a woman. I don't care what you do to me. . . . I'll wear my hair long, I'll give up cigarettes, I'll throw away the books. . . . Just let me be a woman, take me. It's what I want. It's *all* I want. I don't care about anything else" (237). Of course Hella's being a woman rather than a man is, where her relationship with David is concerned, precisely the problem. Her surname, Lincoln, becomes significant in this context—for, like Bartram, she is not an emancipator but a kind of sexual enforcer: "There's a difference between little boys and little girls, just like they say in those little blue books. Little girls want little boys. But little boys—!" (243).

Abraham Lincoln is demythologized in *Giovanni's Room*, and in the process we are given to understand that the social effects of the immensely sophisticated institution of slavery remain with us. Because she finally acknowledges his dilemma ("It's Giovanni . . . he was in love with you" [234, 235]), one might say that Hella frees David, but she also repudiates him: "There are women who have forgotten that to be a woman doesn't simply mean humiliation, doesn't simply mean bitterness. I'm not going to forget it. I'm getting out of this house, away from you, just as fast as taxis, trains, and boats will carry me" (239). In yet another conflation of sexuality and race, Baldwin suggests two things: that the Emancipation Proclamation was a hoax, since African Americans are still fighting for their true liberation; and that acknowledging one's homosexuality (either to oneself or to others) is a queer and painful freedom when there are no safeguards (public or private) for those who dare to declare themselves.

In order for Marcher to achieve the kind of self-knowledge Sedgwick demands, he would have to exist in a culture that has an investment in encouraging latent homosexuals to cast off their masks. In the story's climactic scene, when Marcher visits Bartram's grave, he is captivated by a middle-aged man in deep mourning:

> This face, one grey afternoon when the leaves were thick in the alleys, looked into Marcher's own, at the cemetery, with an expression like the cut of a blade. He felt it, that is, so deep down that he winced at the steady thrust. The person who so mutely assaulted him was a figure he had noticed, on reaching his own

goal, absorbed by a grave a short distance away, a grave apparently fresh, so that the emotion of the visitor would probably match it for frankness. (532–33)

If we follow James's map obediently, then the significance of this encounter is clear: Marcher is stunned by the mourner's involuntary grief, is devastated by his own memory of a relationship that did not produce a similar response in him. "No passion," we are told, "had ever touched him, for this was what passion meant; he had survived and maundered and pined, but where had been *his* deep ravage?" (534). But such an approach does not account for the suggestion of an impropriety (or at the very least of a misunderstanding) on Marcher's part—and perhaps on the mourner's as well. Can we infer that Marcher has behaved indecorously by exhibiting too obvious an interest in another man's loss? Or does the mourner instantly identify Marcher's throbbing "ache," "the steady thrust," as homosexual desire itself? Does the mourner reprove Marcher for his "frankness"—accuse him, in effect, of a subtle but nevertheless indecent exposure? Or perhaps the confrontation represents a brief moment of mutually manifest desire, but one in which neither party is able or willing to break the silence. In the presence of this man, Marcher is aware of a "kind of hunger in his look" (533), is "conscious . . . of something that profaned the air" (534); what is more, he is suddenly "roused, startled, shocked" (534). In short, because Victorian sentimentality, and by extension conventions of heterosexual romance, are under critique throughout the text, Marcher's dilemma may have less to do with the fact that his relationship with Bartram was not a love affair than with what is at stake when one takes a tentative step out of the closet. Clearly, Sedgwick is interested in rescuing Bartram from her cultural prison, with the result that Marcher's incarceration is trivialized: ". . . John Marcher becomes, in this reading, not the finally self-knowing man who is capable of heterosexual love, but the irredeemably self-ignorant man who embodies and enforces heterosexual compulsion. . . . What is strikingly open in the ending of 'The Beast in the Jungle' is how central . . . is man's desire for man—and the denial of that desire."[17]

Of course, James never names Marcher's beast; instead, we are left to speculate on the implications of the "pang" (534), the "anguish of inward throbs" (534), the yearning for (emotional?) penetration. Since the sensations the mourner stirs in Marcher present themselves as Marcher contemplates Bartram's grave, there is the temptation to hand the matter over to Girard and be done with it. But, within this triangular configuration, who is the subject, the object, the mediator?

David's brief encounter with a sailor—so evocative of James's graveyard scene—provides a fuller indication of how Baldwin may have read the story. "Younger . . . , blonder and more beautiful," the sailor, we are told, "wore his masculinity as unequivocally as he wore his skin" (133); David, "staring at him" (133), is like Marcher both transfixed and convinced that he has betrayed himself through "some all-revealing panic . . . in [his] eyes" (134). In this scene Baldwin reaffirms David's thorough cultural conditioning. For how else do we account for his self-loathing and sense of inadequacy before this seemingly overpowering and representative maleness? Succumbing to the notion that homosexuals can only parody heterosexuals, David sets up a classic power imbalance in which he is the transmuted object (the woman) whose only commodity within the marketplace of desire is his (her) youth—which he initially attempts to sell to the sailor. This is, in part, why he likens his gaze to that of a "desperately well-dressed nymphomaniac or trollop who was trying to make him believe she was a lady" (134).

But the sailor, giving him a "look contemptuously lewd and knowing" (134), isn't buying:

> And in another second, had our contact lasted, I was certain that
> there would erupt into speech, out of all that light and beauty,

some brutal variation of *Look, baby, I know you.* I felt my face flame,
I felt my heart harden and shake as I hurried past him, trying to
look stonily beyond him. . . . I got to the other side of the boule-
vard, not daring to look back, and I wondered what he had seen
in me to elicit such instantaneous contempt. (134)

Just as he commodifies desire, so David also expresses the deeply
felt and equally bourgeois conviction that to live as a homosexual
is to forfeit masculinity. The further pathology of this encounter
involves the sailor's heightened allure in David's eyes precisely
because he is a cliché—a "real" man, a heterosexual homophobe—and is therefore by definition unattainable.

David finally concludes that "what the sailor had seen in . . .
[his] unguarded eyes was envy *and* [my emphasis] desire" (135).
If indeed Baldwin throws James's sexual subtext into relief, he also
suggests that the social desire to be "inside," as David says, to
enjoy the privileges and the legitimacy extended to the nonmar-
ginalized as a matter of course, is as powerful as the psychic need
to overcome one's repressions. Nevertheless, resigning itself to,
rather than redefining, the beast, *Giovanni's Room* forces David outside—"[t]he morning weigh[ing] on [his] shoulders with the
dreadful weight of hope" (248).

Strangers in the Village

Is there any terrestrial paradise where, amidst the whispering of the olive-leaves, people can be with whom they like and have what they like and take their ease in shadows and in calmness? Or are all men's lives . . . broken, tumultuous, agonized, and unromantic . . . , periods punctuated by screams, by imbecilities, by deaths, by agonies? Who the devil knows?
Ford Madox Ford

And, of course, many of us have become, in effect, commuters; which is a less improbable state now than it was a decade ago. Many have neither returned nor stayed, but can be found in the Village bars, talking about Europe, or in European bars, talking about America.
James Baldwin

Stranger's Return

A generation ago Addison Gayle dismissed Baldwin as an assimilationist, arguing of "Stranger in the Village," a signature essay and the focus of this chapter, that its "obsession with fusing the black and white cultures—even at the risk of destroying the black—is . . . pervasive. . . ."[1] Indeed, in the late 1960s, Baldwin was for several black intellectuals a highly problematic figure. Some, like Harold Cruse, were appalled by his unapologetic Eurocentrism and, in the midst of what looked to be a social revolution in need of all the black troops it could muster, dismayed by his refusal to take up permanent residence in America. Still others, like Eldridge Cleaver, were unable to forgive him for his homosexuality.

In *The Crisis of the Negro Intellectual,* Cruse railed against Baldwin's objection to the classification of black writer: "[W]hile desiring only to be accepted as a writer (and not necessarily as a Negro writer at that), [Baldwin] takes himself seriously as a Negro spokesman. But a Negro writer cannot, today, make declarations about the need for a 'radical reconstruction' of American society while, at the same time, scoffing at 'sociology and economics of jazz' as not being worth the time of serious study by writers such as himself."[2] Cruse's ultimate conclusion: "Baldwin does not know what he stands for sociologically."[3]

Calling Baldwin a "Stepin Fetchit," Cleaver argued in *Soul on Ice* that his "nose, like the North-seeking needle on a compass, is forever pointed to his adopted fatherland, Europe, his by intellectual osmosis and in Africa's stead."[4] But as I have suggested, this attack was motivated less by a disdain for Baldwin's ostensible politics of assimilation than by a contempt for the homosexual thematics running through his work:

> [I]t seems that many Negro homosexuals, acquiescing in this racial death-wish, are outraged and frustrated because in their sickness they are unable to have a baby with a white man. The cross they have to bear is that, already bending over and touching their toes for the white man, the fruit of their miscegenation is not the little half-white offspring of their dreams but an increase in the unwinding of their nerves—though they redouble their efforts and intake of the white man's sperm.[5]

Gay men yearn for the generative power of women? Alternatively, one might argue that in Baldwin's texts homosexuality comments on the destruction of the African American's filiative bond to Africa. If in Baldwin's view the filiative is no longer possible, then he privileges the affiliative, reminds us again and again, through the figure of the male-male relationship (the emblem of infecundity), that blacks can never reproduce the culture from which they were extracted and therefore must form new associations and alliances. Of course, the problem, for Cleaver and for us, is that the new associations and alliances in question appear to be Western. Why not *affiliate* with Africa?

Were Cleaver writing today, then presumably his homophobia, not to mention his essentialism, would not be tolerated within most progressive intellectual circles. And Baldwin, once expelled from it, has been or is about to be returned to the canon. The first indication of his shifting status came in 1989 with the publication of *James Baldwin: The Legacy*, a random sampling of Baldwin's essays and interviews coupled with elegiac remarks by, among others, Toni Morrison and Amiri Baraka. That same year, *Conversations with James Baldwin* appeared; it included Henry Louis Gates, Jr.'s, 1973 interview with him. Indeed, in the more recent and much discussed "Tell Me, Sir . . . What *Is* Black Literature?,"[6] mapping out the course of black theory for the 1990s, Gates invokes Baldwin twice. His epigraph is taken from "Here Be Dragons":

> [E]ven today, it seems to me (possibly because I am black) very dangerous to model one's opposition to the arbitrary definition, the imposed ordeal, merely on the example supplied by one's oppressor. The object of one's hatred is never, alas, conveniently outside but is seated in one's lap, stirring in one's bowels and dictating the beat of one's heart. And if one does not know this, one risks becoming an imitation—and, therefore, a continuation—of principles one imagines oneself to despise.[7]

Originally published in *Playboy* as "Freaks and the American Ideal of Manhood" in 1965, "Here Be Dragons" is not only among Baldwin's most complicated meditations on whether American blackness is discrete, can be said to exist without reference to American whiteness; it is also his most forthright statement on homosexuality. But Gates falls silent on Baldwin's sexual orientation, even though the quotation with which "Tell Me, Sir" begins so clearly invites us to ponder what makes Baldwin different from, for example, Richard Wright. For as Baldwin has it, the oppressor is "stirring in one's bowels"—an image of rape to which I shall return later. I am suggesting that Gates's avoidance of Baldwin's homopoetics (politics) proceeds from a desire to keep the recanonizing train on track—a train driven by theories of race and writing designed to minimize difference, to promote the academic institutionalization of blackness by homogenizing it.

Later in his essay Gates cites a key passage from Baldwin's "Notes of a Native Son": "I have not written about being a Negro at such length because I expect that to be my only subject, but only because it was the gate I had to unlock before I could hope to write about anything else."[8] Thus Baldwin, the writer whom an earlier generation of black cultural critics had reproved, would be reclaimed by one of the most visible and vocal black theorists writing today. But in recanonizing Baldwin, in proclaiming him a misunderstood native son, what are our objectives? Has contemporary theory taught us that Baldwin was right all along, that "blackness" and "whiteness" are arbitrary social categories? My fear is that the new attention Baldwin is receiving is hollow, merely politically fashionable, and perhaps even self-serving.

In a new era of radical chic, reading Baldwin is de rigueur. Trends notwithstanding, we have a responsibility to confront what remains difficult in Baldwin. And what is difficult—as problematic now as it was twenty years ago—involves his unsteady confidence in the African-American ability to reclaim African traditions and literatures, coupled with a pronounced anxiety about the legitimacy of black American culture itself. These difficulties, these anxieties are acute in "Stranger in the Village." But because the essay was published at the beginning of Baldwin's career (in 1953, the same year *Go Tell It on the Mountain* appeared, or roughly ten years before the advent of black studies and nearly thirty years before canon reformation became an intellectual imperative of contemporary progressives), it is perhaps misguided to claim it, as Gayle had done, as representative. And yet it also anticipates Baldwinian ambivalences toward Western culture, in terms of its whiteness and/or its blackness, that one remarks in work as late as "Here Be Dragons."

I have said that in *Tender Is the Night* Fitzgerald pronounced Switzerland the "centre" of the Western world.[9] To the extent that Baldwin's writing about Europe subsumes the discourse of prior white writers who (though of course for different reasons) were

disenchanted with the American scene and thus exiled themselves, Baldwin's village is properly in Switzerland. But any readerly expectation of a revalorization of the European polis is repeatedly denied throughout the essay. The village is "virtually
unknown"[10] and set in a "landscape . . . absolutely forbidding,
mountains towering on all four sides, ice and snow as far as the
eye can reach" (80). Revising, as I suggest in Chapter 1, James's
well-known inventory of what America does not have, Baldwin
writes that in this Swiss hamlet "there is no movie house, no bank,
no library, no theater; very few radios, one jeep, one station
wagon; and, at the moment, one typewriter, mine, an invention
which the woman next door to me here had never seen" (79–80).
Europe in this new figuration is a "white wilderness" (80) populated by people who do not read, write, attend the theater or
cinema, or engage in any sustaining commerce:

> There are four or five hotels, all closed now, and four or five *bistros*,
> of which, however, only two do any business during the winter.
> . . . There are a few stores, butcher, baker, *épicerie*, a hardware store,
> and a money-changer. (80)

The natives are ignorant and thoroughly conditioned. But the
village itself, despite its shortcomings, remains a sacred place, "a
lesser Lourdes" (80), attracting in summer "a disquietingly high
proportion of . . . tourists [who] are cripples, or semicripples, who
come year after year—from other parts of Switzerland, usually—to take the waters" (80). Even when the West is refigured a
waste land, in other words, it nevertheless draws a loyal, if disabled, following:

> There is often something beautiful, there is always something
> awful, in the spectacle of a person who has lost one of his faculties,
> a faculty he never questioned until it was gone, and who struggles
> to recover it. Yet people remain people, on crutches or indeed on

deathbeds; and wherever I passed, the first summer I was here, among the native villagers or among the lame, a wind passed with me—of astonishment, curiosity, amusement, and outrage. (80)

Since "few people making plans for a holiday would elect to come here" (79), why does Baldwin? The village does have the "advantage of being extremely cheap" (80)—a statement in which there is the faint echo of Malcolm Cowley, who suggested that the so-called lost generation, in his view a generation of apolitical pleasure seekers, had sought asylum in Europe out of economic self-interest, out of a desire to live well for less. If "Stranger in the Village" strives to situate itself within the American tradition of exile, it succeeds only partially. Baldwin, it becomes clear, is not Cowley's Hemingway or Fitzgerald transcribed. He is not a white writer in blackface. Instead, he implicitly asks what African Americans who, consciously or unconsciously, retrace the master pattern of exile and return can salvage from the record of their white predecessors.

As Baldwin walks the village streets, "the children shout *Neger! Neger!*" (81). Obsessed with body, they approach the lone black man as they would a beast in a cage:

> Some thought my hair was the color of tar, that it had the texture of wire, or the texture of cotton. It was jocularly suggested that I might let it all grow long and make myself a winter coat. If I sat in the sun for more than five minutes some daring creature was certain to come along and gingerly put his fingers on my hair, as though he were afraid of an electric shock, or put his hand on my hand, astonished that the color did not rub off. (81)

In response to all this, Baldwin—disturbingly accommodating—smiles: "My smile was simply another unheard-of phenomenon which allowed them to see my teeth—they did not, really, see my smile and I began to think that, should I take to snarling, no one would notice any difference" (81). Again, why remain in the village? Moreover, the suggestion that the children's essentialism is somehow innocent, indeed "very different" (81) from the American preoccupation with the physical properties of blackness, becomes yet another obstacle in the attempt to locate ourselves in an essay whose codes may be foreign: "In all of this, in which . . . there was certainly no element of intentional unkindness, there was yet no suggestion that I was human. . . . The children who shout *Neger!* have no way of knowing the echoes this sound raises in me" (81). In short, what is the appropriate response to Baldwin's conciliatory gestures?

If we assume that the societal differences between the early 1950s and the early 1990s are substantial, then we should perhaps approach "Stranger in the Village" as a textual artifact whose signs and references must be relearned. And yet black intellectuals continue to negotiate with white culture; we may simply have discovered new ways of smiling, new ways of shielding ourselves from attack. Despite Baldwin's conclusion that the children who shout do so from within a different historical frame of reference and therefore cannot know that to a black American *"neger"* sounds like "nigger," he is nevertheless unable to re-referentialize the term—no more than he can re-produce the European experience of prior white American writers, who of course were not accosted in the streets every day because of their otherness. The objectification he experiences in Europe, in Switzerland, is finally not different, and thus the essay must re-present America's history of racial oppression, a history that is inescapable.

[T]here are days when I cannot pause and smile, when I have no heart to play with . . . [the children]; when, indeed, I mutter sourly to myself, exactly as I muttered on the streets of a city these children have never seen, when I was no bigger than these children are now: *Your* mother *was a nigger.* Joyce is right about history being a nightmare—but it may be the nightmare from which no one *can* awaken. People are trapped in history and history is trapped in them. (81)

Exiled in his exile, Baldwin transforms the men he encounters in Switzerland into those he had known in America, reminding us in the process of the Western obsession with the sexual threat of blackness:

> [S]ome of the men have accused *le sale nègre*—behind my back—of stealing wood and there is already in the eyes of some of them that peculiar, intent, paranoiac malevolence which one sometimes surprises in the eyes of American white men when, out walking with their Sunday girl, they see a Negro male approach. (85)

The history of slavery is also written into the text. Indeed, the slave is the controlling metaphor of the essay:

> The American Negro slave could not suppose . . . as slaves in past epochs had supposed and often done, that he would ever be able to wrest the power from his master's hands. This was a supposition which the modern era, which was to bring about such vast changes in the aims and dimensions of power, put to death. . . . But even had this supposition persisted with undiminished force, the American Negro slave could not have used it to lend his condition dignity, for the reason that this supposition rests on another: that the slave in exile yet remains related to his past, has some means—if only in memory—of revering and sustaining the forms of his former life, is able, in short, to maintain his identity. (85–86)

Baldwin carefully avoids the cliché of the utterly powerless African-American slave. He suggests instead that American slavery was so thoroughly successful as an institution not simply because African Americans were subjugated under the yoke of an alien culture but also because the ties binding us to Africa were deliberately severed by "the conquerors." Power is understood to be the product of a heritage that has been handed down intact:

> [The American Negro slave] is unique among the black men of the world in that his past was taken from him, almost literally, at one blow. One wonders what on earth the first slave found to say to the first dark child he bore. I am told that there are Haitians able to trace their ancestry back to African kings, but any American Negro wishing to go back so far will find his journey through time abruptly arrested by the signature on the bill of sale which served as the entrance paper for his ancestor. (86)

There is another village in "Stranger in the Village": the ancestral African village, with which Baldwin attempts to reestablish a connection. But the way back to Africa eludes him because white culture always interposes itself.

Even in Switzerland the imprimatur of slavery is bold. Though the villagers insist that they have never seen a black man before, they do participate in what amounts to a slave trade—a Christian crusade for the salvation of African "heathens":

> There is a custom in the village—I am told it is repeated in many villages—of "buying" African natives for the purpose of converting them to Christianity. There stands in the church all year round a small box with a slot for money, decorated with a black figurine, and into this box the villagers drop their francs. During the *carnaval* which precedes Lent, two village children have their faces blackened—out of which bloodless darkness their blue eyes shine like ice—and fantastic horsehair wigs are placed on their blond heads; thus disguised, they solicit among the villagers for money for the missionaries in Africa. Between the box in the church and the blackened children, the village "bought" last year six or eight African natives. . . . I was careful to express astonishment and pleasure at the solicitude shown by the village for the souls of black folk. (82)

Whiteness here, in a paradigmatic moment, is transmuted into blackness—alternately, ambiguously, a trope and a biological fact. The "disguised" children are not of course genetically black; their bodies have been "blackened." But this blackening is in itself quite complicated. It comments on how white culture perceives blackness—which is to say does not perceive it, since the way the children are made to look results from a culturally determined idea of blackness as alien, grotesque, subhuman. The way black people actually look, in other words, is irrelevant. And thus the text points up the inadequacy of conceiving race biologically. On the other hand, however, as we have seen, Baldwin's skin color will not "rub off." This would seem to suggest that blackness is not in his view only a figure, that its physical properties are quite literally essential to defining a black self. How, then, does one read the seemingly crucial sentence that comes later: "When, beneath the black mask, a human being begins to make himself felt one cannot escape a certain awful wonder as to what kind of human being it is" (84)?

Gayle and Cleaver might have argued of writing like this that it merely reaffirms Baldwin's controlling desire to see himself as a white man in blackface: beneath their masks, African Americans are white. Contemporary critics might object to Baldwin's universalism: white or black, beneath our masks we are all the same. But "Stranger in the Village" is more sophisticated, or more slippery, than such readings imply. The children in blackface are indeed masked, "bloodless," figural—but their "blue eyes shin[ing] like ice" work as emblems of miscegenation, the effects of which are cultural *and* biological. Which is not to say, with Gayle and Cleaver, that Baldwin aspires to assimilate into a culture that has rejected him, for aspiration is not at issue. "Stranger in the Village" addresses the consequences of events that African Americans could not control, reenacts "the interracial drama acted out on the American continent." (89).

The complexities of biological miscegenation aside, "Stranger in the Village" points toward a possible textual miscegenation, even a textual rape. Canons and the formation of canons are underlying concerns:

> These people . . . have made the modern world, in effect, even if they do not know it. The most illiterate among them is related, in a way that I am not, to Dante, Shakespeare, Michelangelo, Aeschylus, Da Vinci, Rembrandt, and Racine; the cathedral at Chartres says something to them which it cannot say to me. . . . Out of their hymns and dances come Beethoven and Bach. Go back a few centuries and they are in their full glory—but I am in Africa, watching the conquerors arrive. (83)

In theorizing about the West, Baldwin sees Aeschylus, Dante, Shakespeare, and Racine as representatives of the writers who matter. They are the authorities. But what to do about them? A contemporary theorist would revise the canon. Although I have implied that Baldwin's work anticipates cultural theories we routinely apply today, the conventional view of his early work is that it defers to the patriarchy, advocates mastery. And yet "Stranger in the Village" implicitly asks whether, say, Shakespeare can be rewritten—whether an interpretive strategy privileging blackness is sustainable as one surveys the master texts of the West. In other words, if human beings can be blackened, can a text? The question assumes that blackness is definable, but the Baldwinian dilemma emerges from an inability to ascertain what that quality is. Blackness is, in this essay, ambiguously not whiteness. A fully realized African-American self cannot occur without access to Africa—access to its rituals, to *its* "hymns and dances," and above all to its languages. However, as I have indicated, for Baldwin the journey back to Africa is one in which white writing—"the signature on the bill of sale"—superimposes itself over blackness, over whatever language or languages Baldwin's ancestors may have known. And he does not, and insists that he cannot, know what these languages were.

Positing an uninterrupted continuum between Africa and Afro-America, critics like Gates have recently implored African-American theorists to "turn inward," to concentrate on our own "critical tradition and languages."[11] In "Stranger in the Village," however, Baldwin expresses little confidence in black cultural self-determination because, as he maintains, blacks read and write in a prison-house of language conceived and maintained by whites. In his view the forms African Americans deploy are not "borrowed,"[12] to use Gates's term, for this implies volition and a degree of control; they were imposed on us. We were raped. The discursive result of the violation is not a hybridization of two cultures, an obvious textual half-breed, but a text like "Stranger in the Village," in which the language is "standard" and the structure "classic," in which blackness leaves no trace. If Baldwin suggests that legitimate blackness is African, that legitimate black languages are African, then the African American is illegitimate, and so is the African-American vernacular. African Americans are, in the text, the progeny white culture refuses to recognize. Their vernacular is a function of marginalization: it is a dialect, as opposed to a language. Gayle argues that in "Stranger in the Village" Baldwin worships the "genius, mastery, and artistic superiority of white, Western man."[13] Read in this way, the essay is simply a capitulation to white authority; read as a meditation on cultural captivity, it is intent on repossessing the "genius, mastery, and artistic superiority" of Africa—and cannot.

". . . I . . . find myself among a people," Baldwin writes, "whose culture controls me, has even, in a sense, created me . . ." (82). He is all at once an alien in the West, its product, and an invisible citizen seemingly overwhelmed by the authority of Europe:

> [T]hese people have never seen America, nor have most of them seen more of Europe than the hamlet at the foot of their mountain. Yet they move with an authority which I shall never have; and they regard me, quite rightly, not only as a stranger in their village

but as a suspect latecomer, bearing no credentials, to everything they have—however unconsciously—inherited. For this village, even were it incomparably more remote and incredibly more primitive, is the West . . . onto which I have been so strangely grafted. (83)

On the evidence of "Stranger in the Village," when Baldwin confronts the Master, as James ironically came to be known, he recognizes only half of himself. Still, as a reader he is free to proclaim himself James's disciple, even his son. But this is a rhetorical gesture only. Beyond the text, there are no systems in place encouraging blacks to think of themselves as white people.

"From all available evidence," Baldwin remarks,

no black man had ever set foot in this tiny Swiss village before I came. I was told before arriving that I would probably be a "sight" for the village; I took this to mean that people of my complexion were rarely seen in Switzerland, and also that city people are always something of a "sight" outside of the city. It did not occur to me—possibly because I am an American—that there could be people anywhere who had never seen a Negro. (79)

Assuming that "Stranger in the Village" undertakes a kind of anthropological investigation of a community, then it ends up co-opting the biases and blindnesses undergirding the work of white anthropologists like Malinowski and Mead. The ethnographic transposition is stunning: as Baldwin has it, the "real" savages, the indisputable primitives, are white Europeans. If Marianna Torgovnick is right, then

those who study or write about the primitive usually begin by defining it as different from (usually opposite to) the present.
    After that, reactions to the present take over. Is the present too materialistic? Primitive life is not—it is a precapitalist utopia in which only use value, never exchange value, prevails. Is the pres-

ent repressed? Not primitive life—primitives live life whole, without fear of the body. Is the present promiscuous and undiscriminating sexually? Then primitives teach us the inevitable limits and controls placed on sexuality and the proper subordination of sexuality to the needs of child rearing. Does the present see itself as righteously Christian? Then primitives become heathens, mired in false beliefs. Does the present include vigorous business expansion? Then primitives cease to be thought of as human and become a resource for industry, able to work mines and supply natural wealth. In each case, the needs of the present determine the value and nature of the primitive. The primitive does what we ask it to do. Voiceless, it lets us speak for it.[14]

Torgovnick, of course, is concerned with white mythologies of the primitive, with white culture's investment in defining itself against them. By virtue of his blackness, Baldwin is in Western terms a representative savage, but he obviously is not "voiceless." To name the bracket in which the West has enclosed African Americans is to begin to escape it. Détente, intricate negotiations with the hegemony, are not the only political strategies operating in the text. Proclaiming that these people "have cost me more in anguish and rage than they will ever know" (82), Baldwin retaliates—primitivizing whiteness, transforming the exalted Western "we" into a discredited "them."

At the end of his first sojourn in the village, Baldwin had resolved "never . . . to return" (80). And yet he does, the following winter, "to work" (80). But the nature of the project, the writerly task he sets himself, is various. It is at times anthropological (an attempt "to know who the white man is" [84]), at others almost messianic, and at still others surprisingly militant. The "work" is ultimately a cultural enterprise marked by the implication of coercion, by the suggestion that the stranger inhabits (writes and writes in) the village, which he insists "is the West" (83), against his will. I began by asking why Baldwin would choose to remain in so alienating a place, but the question misses the point: namely, that there is nowhere else to go.

6

Writing the American Scene:
James and Baldwin,
James/Baldwin, James Baldwin

"American writers do not have a fixed society to describe. The only society they know is one in which nothing is fixed and in which the individual must fight for his identity."[1] Like James before him, Baldwin insists that America is a nonplace and that one's identity as an American is to be found only in Europe. Though exiles both, Baldwin and James are obviously exiled from each other: by generation, class, race—by the way their contemporaries understood and received their work, and of course by the very canons to which they are assigned today. And yet both construe America as a spatial and, coextensively, as a sociopolitical impossibility. And both, moreover, see New York as the city that best illustrates their disaffection from the country at large. Beginning with a reading of *The American Scene*, this chapter then considers three essays in which James's impressionistic chronicle of American mores is Baldwin's clear if unspoken preoccupation: "The Discovery of What It Means to Be an American," "Fifth Avenue, Uptown," and "East River, Downtown."

Suggesting that American modernist autobiographies systematically reproduce the very spatial disintegration they find so repellent, William Boelhower maintains that the act of duplicating the "phantasmagoria" precipitates a crisis; namely, the inability to incarnate "a rarefied world of process which has a beginning but no end," a world where "intellect dominates at the expense of sentiment and senses, and the very idea of body is forgotten."[2] In the "nostalgia for an asylum, for a proper dwelling," the modernist autobiographer opposes the American metropolis ("cubist," "cinematic," dystopian) to the European polis ("perspectivist," "photographic," utopian).[3] Boelhower's point, of course, is that for the narratives in question this binarism is unstable and ultimately unenforceable.

The same frustration, the same yearning for an "asylum" imagined as European, energizes *The American Scene*, even if technically it is not a modernist text. For James represents himself as a "survivor scrambling out of the current and up the bank" of the life-threatening experience of New York.[4] On Wall Street he is at the "wide edge of the whirlpool" (80). Before the Waldorf Astoria, the "force of the breaking public wave" (100) washes over him. But it is from the Hudson that the city is at its most

> extravagant . . . , imparting to every object and element, to the motion and expression of every floating, hurrying, panting thing, to the throb of ferries and tugs, to the plash of waves and the play of winds and the glint of lights and the shrill whistles and the quality and authority of breeze-borne cries—all practically, a diffused, wasted clamour of *detonations*—something of its sharp free accent and, above all, its sovereign sense of being "backed" and able to back. (74–75)

New York, then, is boundaryless, without limits. And yet in this city of "motion" and flux there remains an "old inconceivably bourgeois scheme of composition and distribution . . ." (101).

Inconceivable though it may be, there is a "layout," one that does violence to the idea that "we" are in uncharted terrain: "This original sin of the longitudinal avenues perpetually, yet meanly intersected . . . might still have earned forgiveness by some occasional departure from its pettifogging consistency" (101). This is the territory of lawyers and bankers—the princes of capitalism. New York, as James has it, is no longer a phantasmagoria, but an exacting rhetorical design, one that subverts the language of natural (national) disaster to which I have just pointed: "current," "whirlpool," "breaking public wave."

The discursive shift from the glaringly naturalist to the avowedly reified marks the anticapitalist (but also anti-Marxist) underpinnings of James's rhetorical assault on the "new" New York. And thus the famous figure of the skyscraper "piercing" the sky is first inscribed and then castrated, feminized, reduced to a vulgar toiletry on a bourgeois dressing table. Skyscrapers are transformed into a "colossal hair-comb turned upward" (139) or into "extravagant pins in a cushion already overpopulated" (76). But James's attempt to accommodate these buildings as a writer by turning them into a woman's personal effects only underscores his frustration with a social scene in which women are beginning to behave like men, in which the drawing room and the office are virtually one and the same. New York, he maintains, is a city disturbingly free of boundaries of any kind, as is the country at large, figured as a house in which "no one of . . . [the] indoor parts [is] distinguishable from any other" (166). "The diffused vagueness of separation between apartments," he continues, "between hall and room, between one room and another, between the one you are in and the one you are not in, between the place of passage and place of privacy, is a provocation to despair which the public institution shares impartially with the luxurious 'home' " (166).

The absence of designated boundaries—"the effacement of difference," the nonexistence of "background," "limit," and "localizing fact" (167)—is symptomatic of the "social tone that has dictated" homogeneity: "thus we have the law fulfilled that every part of every house shall be, as nearly as may be, visible, visitable, penetrable, not only from every other part, but from as many parts of as many other houses as possible, if they only be near enough" (167). But, as will become clear, this lamentable "efface-ment of difference" is precisely what is desired when "ethnics" are James's subject.

In Chapter 1, I refer to James's keen sense of an unraveling "Anglo-Saxon total." The phrase appears in a letter to his brother William, in which he states that "the melting together [of England and America] will come the faster the more one takes for granted and treats the life of the two countries as continuous or more or less convertible, or at any rate as simply different chapters of the same general subject. . . ."[5] The relation between America and Europe, then, is represented as symbiotic: "continuous" and "con-vertible." But what is important about this epistolary fragment is its clear reliance on the figure of the melting pot. The smooth "melting together" of the Old World and the New is easily ac-complished; however, in this private moment, James falls silent on the issue of ethnicity. And so, in the conclusion to "The Dis-covery of What It Means to Be an American," does Baldwin, who, in reclaiming the Master, essays the same cultural fusion. There is no re-vision, no re-voicing of James, only quotation: Baldwin tells us that his, too, is an "endeavor to wed the vision of the Old World with that of the New" (176). And yet the values Baldwin assigns to these worlds are radically different.

What James did not say to his brother he fully articulates in *The American Scene:* the "English-American world" is about to pull apart due to the "monstrous presumptuous interest . . . [of] the aliens" (86). In 1904 the European presence in America—"the land of the 'open door' " (62)—was never more visible. Since throughout the text James argues that America is not Europe, when clearly in some senses it is, this is especially ironic. James recoils at more than the unrelenting infusion of "foreigners." He is alarmed by the ubiquity of a particular kind of stranger: southern and eastern European peasants. In their American incarnation, the Italians, Jews, and Armenians who had recently "conquered" New York offer a stark contrast to the urbane "white ethnics"—for example, Prince Amerigo, Prince Casamassima, Miriam Rooth—one typically encounters in James's major fiction. If in the novel he labors to keep the lower-class "ethnic" out, in *The American Scene* he abandons the drawing room and roams the streets.

In the introduction to his edition of *The American Scene*, Leon Edel expends a great deal of energy defending James's ethnographic biases, arguing in essence that we should applaud him for his willingness to venture into the Jewish ghetto and commend him for attempting to converse with Italian workers. To F. O. Matthiessen's mild (though risky) suggestion that in his meditation on modern America James "drifted dangerously close to racism," Edel replies: "The book provides no warrant for so strange a conclusion."[6] Edel's resounding "no" hardly satisfies the desire to know more about James's admittedly polyvalent preoccupation with ethnicity, a preoccupation that intensifies when he confronts the African American. With one crucial exception (which I shall discuss later), it is true that James avoids African Americans in the New York sections of the text; they come into play later, when the "restless analyst" ventures south. In Florida he remarks upon the incompetence of the new (free) black servant class and evinces an undeniable nostalgia for the "old Southern tradition," when "the house [was] alive with the scramble of young darkies for the honour of fetching and carrying . . ." (423). Romanticizing the Old South, summoning the ghost of a darky past, James tells us that he could have "shed tears" (423) for the conditions with which "the old planters, the cotton gentry" (423) must now contend: ". . . for *this* they had fought and fallen" (423).

Edel would seem to suggest that despite James's obvious valorization of the antebellum South, Matthiessen's claim is insupportable. Readerly discomfort with James's romantic rhetoric of loss falls away, we are informed, when we recall that in assessing the New South James also paid homage to Du Bois's *Souls of Black Folk*:

> How can everything so have gone that the only "Southern" book of any distinction published for many a year is *The Souls of Black Folk*, by that most accomplished of members of the negro [sic] race, Mr. W. E. B. Du Bois? Had the *only* focus of life then been Slavery?—from the point onward that Slavery had reached a quarter of a century before the War, so that with the extinction of that interest none other of any sort was left. (418)

How to read this brings together much of what I have been attempting to argue thus far, for clearly *it is* significant that James did not ignore this seminal text, especially since his white intellectual contemporaries, as Arnold Rampersad points out, generally did.[7] Still, Du Bois understood slavery negatively, arguing that it "classed the black man and the ox together"[8]; James, however, calls slavery an "interest." And, presumably, he refers to the interest(s) of Southern whites. Given the racist context in which the encomium occurs, reading it as an affirmation of the Master's egalitarianism seems perverse. A resisting reader might argue that James's laudatory assessment suggests that he saw Du Bois as a great exception among a people who had failed to make much of a cultural contribution. And why the quotation marks circumscribing "Southern"? Do they acknowledge that Du Bois was not a native southerner (he was born in Massachusetts), or does James imply that the South is in such a state of chaos that its voice has been usurped by a black man? Or, worse, does he suggest that blacks who presume to publish books only demonstrate that the Civil War was a cultural travesty? The point: that readers of *The American Scene* have generally been oblivious to such questions. On the whole, James's perspective on Southern blacks focuses on their post-Emancipation inability to provide proper service and on how they look, behave, and speak: "They . . . were, as to facial character, vocal tone, primal rawness of speech, general accent and attitude, extraordinarily base and vulgar . . ." (424).

"The Negroes," Edel reports, "scarcely figure in this book; they were not, like the Jews or Italians, to be observed as yet in their Northern slums and had but reached an intermediate stage between slavery and their present militancy."[9] This remark is at once telling and inaccurate. The fact that Edel's edition was released in 1968—a year in which racial turmoil, racial panic, was a daily occurrence—should not be discounted. Indeed, writing at a time when the establishment was under attack once again, Edel declared *The American Scene* essential reading: "Now . . . we can see that in fundamental matters there has been little change in America, only an accentuation of the confusion, distortion, and fragmentation James discerned."[10] But in his haste to reclaim the Master as a cultural oracle, Edel overlooked, or simply had no knowledge of, key statistics.

As David Levering Lewis points out in *When Harlem Was in Vogue*, beginning in the 1890s southern blacks were migrating to San Juan Hill and to the Tenderloin—to, in short, mid-Manhattan. In fact, in 1900 a bloody riot erupted between African Americans and Irish-American workers.[11] According to the United States Census Bureau, 23,601 African Americans were living in New York in 1890; by 1900, 60,666; and by 1910, just six years after James's visit, 91,709.[12] So if blacks were a decided presence in turn-of-the-century Manhattan, then James's failure to mention their burgeoning community is at least as puzzling as Edel's commentary on the omission. There may be a simple explanation for this critical inattentiveness, one that Myra Jehlen helps us construct when she explains what rises to the surface of a text when the critical lens is gender: "One has to read for gender; unless it figures explicitly in story or poem, it will seldom read for itself."[13] I would argue that the same is true of race. Indeed, perhaps the real point is that one has to *want* to read for gender, for race.

Even a poststructuralist critic like Boelhower ends up concurring with Edel; he, too, understands James as a liberal pluralist. The Master's encounter with a group of silent southern Italian "ditchers" is in Boelhower's account symptomatic of James's own sense of displacement and of his thwarted desire to come to terms with difference.[14] Accustomed to lively discourse among Italian workers (in Italy), James is shocked by the lack of exchange, by the absence of camaraderie, in America. The implication is strong that the workers are unable to communicate with each other because they have no common language. Some may have emigrated from Sicily; others from regions where Italian predominates. Boelhower understands this moment of alienation, of defamiliarization, as a comment on James's disgust with the dehumanization of the new immigrants. But James expresses little interest in the reasons behind the massive immigration he witnesses. The idea that the men in question may have found life in Italy intolerable does not appear to have occurred to the Master, who reminds us that the "oncoming" so-called ethnic is at the "stage of his no longer being for you—for any complacency of the romantic, or even verily of the fraternizing sense in you—the foreigner of the quality, of the kind, that he might have been *chez lui*" (127).

The argument that *The American Scene* ultimately attests to James's anachronistic multiculturalist sensibility weakens considerably when one turns to the commonplace racial slurs punctuating the text. These would seem to indicate that James neither resisted nor finally questioned the racial (racist) status quo. Describing the physical features of the "foreigners" he encounters in the streetcars, he remarks that "face after face, unmistakably was 'low' " (126). The images associated with the new immigrant accentuate the unkempt, even the squalid: "Is not the universal sauce essentially *his* sauce, and do we not feel ourselves feeding, half the time, from the ladle, as greasy as he chooses to leave it for us, that he holds out?" (117–18).

One never has the sense that James calls for radical social reform in the way that, say, Lincoln Steffens does in *The Shame of the*

Cities (1904). Instead, and not surprisingly, his discourse compares with that of his haute bourgeois contemporary and friend Edith Wharton. Consider, for example, the Darwinian classifications foregrounded in *The House of Mirth*. Lily Bart, physically the archetypal Anglo-Saxon woman, stands on a higher ethnic rung than Rosedale, "a plump rosy man of the blond Jewish type" endowed "with that mixture of artistic sensibility and business astuteness which characterizes his race."[15] Mrs. Haffen—the ubiquitous, ethnically ambiguous, disfigured charwoman—is literally at Lily's feet and is systematically associated in the text with stairs, with hierarchies. Similarly, "ethnics" in *The American Scene*, especially Jews, are at the bottom of the social order; yet they are as much a threat to the native's authority and privilege as Rosedale or Mrs. Haffen is to Lily's: "So the denizens of the New York ghetto, heaped as thick as the splinters on the table of a glass-blower, had each, like the fine glass particle, his or her individual share of the whole hard glitter of Israel" (132).

Though James admits that the country can and will absorb the "ethnics," the "ingurgitated," he implies that the cost will be high. "There are categories of foreigners, truly, meanwhile," he writes,

> of whom we are moved to say that only a mechanism working with scientific force could have performed the feat of making them colourless. The Italians who, over the whole land, strike us, I am afraid, as, after the Negro and the Chinaman, the human value most easily produced, the Italians meet us, at every turn, only to make us ask what has become of that element of the agreeable address in *them* which has, from far back, so enhanced for the stranger the interest and pleasure of a visit to their beautiful country. (128)

In the New York chapters this is the sole allusion to African Americans. We have moved beyond the metaphor of the melting pot to a more powerful figure, one capable of bleaching out, of erasing, color altogether. The yearning for the "colourless" perhaps explains why James is noticeably silent on African-American communities in Manhattan: blackness, when mixed with whiteness, is indelible and therefore unspeakable. He can envision an "amalgam" consisting of Anglo-Saxons and visibly white "ethnics," but James is unable to entertain the possibility of a physical commingling involving brown Sicilians, yellow Asians, or blacks. But how to interpret the curious phrase "most easily produced"? And why is James "afraid"? Given what he says about the superabundance of Jews in New York—about the "ubiquity of . . . their children" (132), about their being "there for race, and not, as it were, for reason" (132), about "the gathered past of Israel mechanically pushing through" (132)—James could easily mean by "produced" reproduced, thus accounting for the linguistic shudder undergirding the mere mention of these people of color who (are we to infer?) will eventually take over.

Those who privilege James's formalism may find such speculation unfair, peculiarly callous. After all, *The American Scene* is his construction. He brings to bear upon the figure of America, in other words, the full weight of his narrative mastery. The deft movement from North to South, for example, is a compelling, if problematic, attempt to recover, quite literally, the Union. But even if we think of this text as a well-wrought fiction, how do we account for its acute interest in what Philip Fisher calls "hard facts," those signal historical moments that literature not only reproduces but also inserts, through the very act of re-presentation, into culture? Fisher's facts—the Native American slaughter, slavery, and urban expansion—provide the framework for his analysis of Cooper, Stowe, and Dreiser.[16] There are of course other hard facts—among them early-twentieth-century immigration and the challenge it presented (as far as nativists were concerned) to America's ethnic continuity. So, though some readers may want to insist that *The American Scene* is a kind of impressionistic novel (and, of course, such readers would also have to say that novels have nothing to do with history), there are reasons to explore why Italians, Jews, Asians, and blacks are marked in the text. But as I have suggested, the decision to undertake such an investigation is finally a question of political desire and (to reinvoke Jehlen) of white male privilege, too—arguably, only readers who are in power or who yearn for power exercise the privilege of defending or excusing or ignoring James's blindnesses and prejudices. And yet the paradox of Baldwin's discipleship is that it must have involved similar tactics, similar misreadings.

The reluctance to address James's racism, or at best his nativism, can be related to another silence that one so often finds in the scholarship: the extent to which a homoerotics of desire informs his work. Critical racism and critical homophobia, in other words, may go hand in hand. Arguing that there is a "repressive blankness" when it comes to the discussion of homosexual desire, in his narratives and in his life, Eve Sedgwick suggests in *Epistemology of the Closet* that critics have been

> motivated . . . by a desire to protect James from homophobic misreadings in a perennially repressive sexual climate. It is possible that they fear that, because of the asymmetrically marked structure of heterosexist discourse, *any* discussion of homosexual desires or literary content will marginalize him (or them?) as, simply *homosexual*. It is possible that they desire to protect him from anachronistically gay readings, based on a late twentieth-century vision of men's desire for men that is more stabilized and culturally compact than James's own.[17]

The conservative critical need to safeguard James's house of narrative from invasion by what some would call anachronistically ethnic readings is as strong as the urge to shield his work from approaches demanding a closer scrutiny of the homoerotic. This impulse to silence, really to reprimand, is inextricably bound up with the depoliticizing (heterosexualizing) idea that a "great"

writer is also a "great" man—always endowed with a universaliza-
ble vision. Since readers of Baldwin are less timid about discussing
either his homosexuality or his views on race—even when they
risk being understood to say that homosexuality and racial conflict are the only traceable patterns in his work—the "protection"
James commands becomes somewhat mysterious. The comparative readerly openness characterizing the criticism of Baldwin
may in fact reflect certain institutionally embedded assumptions
about who reads whom. The implicit message within the profession today—despite the advent of groundbreaking criticism like
Men in Feminism, Engendering Men, "Race," Writing, and Difference, or,
indeed, *Epistemology of the Closet*—is that writing about race, gender,
and sexual orientation is a worthy enterprise, as long as conventional boundaries are dutifully enforced. Gay people, allegedly,
are at their theoretical best when they read gay texts; women,
when they read women; blacks, when they focus their attention
on other blacks.

But when reading Baldwin in relation to James, or James in
relation to Baldwin, the consoling categories upon which the
academy still heavily relies become obstacles in themselves. Sedgwick argues that critics quite possibly "read James himself, as in
his work, positively refusing or evaporating . . . [the] element of
his eros, translating lived homosexual desires, where he had them,
into written heterosexual ones so thoroughly and so successfully
that the difference *makes* no difference, the transmutation leaves
no residue."[18] If Sedgwick is right and James was a masterful trans-
lator of sexual desire, then did his ability to perform transforma-
tive feats extend beyond eros? For there are occasions in *The American Scene* when he does indeed write as though free of the
cognitive limitations of "ordinary" men, does indeed achieve a
transmutation in which a liberal, eminently civilized voice, sometimes sustained for pages at a time, becomes so seductive, so powerful, that we forget (or want to forget) about the racial slurs,
the cultural sterotypes, the unapologetic nostalgia for the "Anglo-

Saxon total." Given Baldwin's undeniable attraction to the cosmo-
politan, his willingness to yield to what for him must have been
the necessary fiction that all are welcome at James's symposium,
that a chair had been reserved for him in the salon, begins to
make a kind of sense.

There can only be speculation here, but, acknowledging his
demonstrable (albeit ultimately inconsistent) liberalism, Baldwin
almost certainly gave James the benefit of the doubt. And yet
there is also the question of what James may have represented to
a young homosexual hungry for "culture." Perhaps like that of no
other American male writer, James's was a life of insistent and
public bachelorhood, a way of life that essentially breaks all the
cultural rules in its rejection of filiative bonds. Electing marginalization, James would have been attractive to a writer who understood himself as marginalized in virtually every sense. And further, it may well be the case that Baldwin, like Sedgwick herself,
was attuned to James's skill at making homosexual desire appear
heterosexual. In short, Baldwin may have recognized in James's
work all the symptoms of homosexual panic. And certainly much
of Baldwin's work is an exercise in translation as well.

Assuming that in his attempt to situate himself within the
American tradition of exile, if only temporarily, Baldwin could
not avoid James, then his essays on New York can be read less as
journalistic exposés of an actual city than as readings of the New
York with which his white precursors were in some senses wholly
preoccupied and wholly determined to escape. But, in the act
of reading James reading New York, Baldwin foregrounds fixed
boundaries as opposed to perpetual flux. The Harlem housing
project dominating the discursive scene in "Fifth Avenue, Uptown" is "on the rehabilitated side of the avenue."[19] "The other
side of the avenue," we are told, "looks exactly as it looked in the
days when we sat with our noses pressed against the windowpane,
longing to be allowed to go 'across the street' " (205). Cutting a
life for himself from Malcolm Cowley's master pattern of "exile

and return," Baldwin has finally received permission "to go 'across the street' "—all the way, in fact, to Paris. Heathcliff transmogrified, Heathcliff "rehabilitated"—he has traversed the threshold of the "windowpane" and entered the cultural big house. Apparently, his sojourn abroad has afforded him the freedom that James takes for granted: to move about the city unchecked. He writes as if detached from the residents of the housing project; he is at a remove from, indeed, able to pass by, the "Jewish proprietor." In this instance, Baldwin assumes the Jamesian role of "analyst," of dispassionate observer. But this is a pose he is unable to sustain. Though James, survivor and enforcer, simultaneously "documents" and transforms the spatial absurdities of New York, it becomes clear that Baldwin, like the people he describes, is "struggling" in the city's "fishhooks," is enmeshed in "the barbed wire" (206).

James, we know, sees conspicuous consumption in New York as the inevitable symptom of democracy's fatal disease. But this anticapitalistic scorn is, of course, a function of his own privilege. In "Fifth Avenue" Baldwin reaffirms James's "bourgeois scheme of composition and distribution," but only to confirm that the racial outsider is also an economic outsider. Critiquing the Black Muslim mandate "to cease trading with white men and establish a separate economy" (206), Baldwin insists that such a strategy is inconceivable "since Negroes do not own General Motors or RCA or the A & P, nor, indeed, do they own more than a wholly insufficient fraction of anything else in Harlem" (206). Calling into question his own success, his own authority and status as a black man who has "made it," Baldwin challenges the Jamesian idea of New York as a spatial economy in which the alien, potentially, negotiates with and even surpasses the native.

The Master's aristocratic condescension has been transformed into outrage at the imbalances and inequities that American capitalism permits. The essay calls for revolution, for far-reaching social changes from which both blacks and whites would benefit. "That hundreds of thousands of white people," Baldwin writes, "are living, in effect, no better than the 'niggers' is not a fact to be regarded with complacency" (208). This is a bold break with Jamesian elitism, for in Baldwin's view the tragedy of America is not its classlessness but rather its classism *and* its racism. And he takes no comfort in the exceptions to whom those who delude themselves into believing that America is a democracy conveniently point:

> The people, however, who believe that this democratic anguish has some consoling value are always pointing out that So-and-So, white, and So-and-So, black, rose from the slums into the big time. The existence—the public existence—of, say, Frank Sinatra and Sammy Davis, Jr., proves to them that America is still the land of opportunity and that inequalities vanish before the determined will. (208)

I have argued that in the late 1960s and early 1970s Baldwin was often misunderstood as the Sammy Davis, Jr., of black intellectuals, as a desperate assimilationist. But in "Fifth Avenue" Baldwin suggests neither that he has achieved in America the status of citizen (which is to say consumer) nor that this is his ambition; he is instead among the consumed: "One," he writes, "is victimized, economically, in a thousand ways—rent, for example, or car insurance. Go shopping one day in Harlem—for anything—and compare Harlem prices and quality with those downtown" (208). Though Baldwin is not unfamiliar with the "downtown" world, has done some comparative shopping, he also insists—in "East River, Downtown," the postscript to "Fifth Avenue, Uptown"—that he is an intruder there:

> Usually . . . white people who are in favor of integration prove to be in favor of it later, in some other city, some other town, some other building, some other school. . . . Negroes know how little most white people are prepared to implement their words with deeds, how little, when the chips are down, they are prepared to

risk. And this long history of moral evasion has had an unhealthy effect on the total life of the country, and has eroded whatever respect Negroes may once have felt for white people.[20]

Baldwin's remarkable essays on New York invite a reconsideration of what it means to write about African-American literature today—especially since reading (writing) blackness now commands the attention of so many white theorists. In "East River" Baldwin suggests that black Americans are finally just like white Americans: "Unless one takes refuge in the theory—however disguised—that Negroes are, somehow, different from white people, I do not see how one can escape the conclusion that the Negro's status in this country is not only a cruel injustice but a grave national liability" (264). This is a statement that Zora Neale Hurston, in vogue in white contemporary theory, could easily have written. I am thinking of her "How It Feels to Be Colored Me" and, more particularly, of Barbara Johnson's elegant, though rather troubling, response to it. In Johnson's reading, Hurston is "a threshold figure mediating between the all-black town of Eatonville, Florida, and the big road traveled by passing whites."[21] Hurston demonstrates that "the moment there is a juxtaposition of black and white, what 'comes' is color. But the colors that come . . . are skin *paint*, not skin complexion. . . . The move into the jungle is a move into mask; the return to civilization is a return to veneer. Either way, what is at stake is an artificial, ornamental surface."[22] On these terms the "insider becomes an outsider the minute she steps out of the inside."[23] If Johnson can turn herself into a black woman, then Baldwin can re-create himself a white man; in fact, as I have argued, he does as much in *Giovanni's Room*. But whether Baldwin finally understands blackness as mere "veneer" is another matter.

As a child, he writes in "East River,"

[o]ne's hair was always being attacked with hard brushes and combs and Vaseline: it was shameful to have "nappy" hair. One's

legs and arms and face were always being greased, so that one
would not look "ashy" in the wintertime. One was always being
mercilessly scrubbed and polished, as though in the hope that a
stain could thus be washed away. . . . The women were forever
straightening . . . their hair, and using bleaching creams. And yet
it was clear that none of this effort would release one from the
stigma and danger of being a Negro. (267–68)

Then blackness is not effaceable, is not mask. Johnson not only
reconfigures Hurston a white woman in blackface but she also
depoliticizes her—ignores "what is at stake" when the African
American assumes the role of mediator with the white world. And
what is at stake is the freedom to get off the metaphorical fence,
to abandon the margin and thus the marginalization—"to go
'across the street.' " When Baldwin argues that there is no difference between black Americans and white Americans, he reminds
us that black people would like to be able to "get a lousy cup of
coffee" (266), would like to enjoy the privileges of full citizenship
that are Johnson's purely because of her whiteness. This is dangerous territory. I do not want to revalorize the biological, nor do I
want to suggest that the physical "fact" of blackness, as opposed
to the way white culture interprets and ultimately disciplines
blackness, is the problem. And yet at the same time it is difficult
to know what the black hand guiding my pen signifies. The physical properties of blackness Baldwin inscribes—the " 'nappy' hair,"
the "stain"—whites, he would seem to claim, generally do not
possess. And for him, moreover, these neither can nor should be
"washed away."

Paris, Baldwin tells us, allows African Americans to discover
themselves because "it is easier to cut across social and occupa-
tional lines there than it is here" (173). James figures New York
as a space where social hierarchies do not exist. And yet, in the
attempt to enforce the binarisms of native/alien, bourgeois/prole-
tarian, polis/metropolis, and, by implication, white/black, he ends

up collapsing them in order to dramatize the chaos that ensues when monoculturalism capitulates to pluralism. The static social order that James understands as European is for Baldwin, paradoxically, certifiably American. In *The American Scene* the "ethnic" working class is the harbinger of a new and ugly social reality. In the multiculturalist design of "Discovery," James's workers—now waiters, actors, "pimps and prostitutes in Pigalle" (174), "Egyptian bankers in Neuilly" (174)—are not only reconfigured; they are recentered and rehumanized.

Writing Paris as the place where hierarchy is a given, Baldwin, who is not of Paris, is free to "reach out to everyone" (174) and to experience for the first time the feeling that "he is accessible to everyone and open to everything" (174). The gap separating him from James (who, though he shuns the "accessible," is able nonetheless to claim the privilege of accessibility whenever he so chooses) suddenly becomes insurmountable. The desire to penetrate territories that in New York are for blacks finally impenetrable forces Baldwin, dispossessed native son, to write America from a distance.

In *Another Country*

Since it brings together so many of the issues undergirding the discourse of exile, and since it is perhaps Baldwin's most ambitious effort, *Another Country* is the text with which I will conclude. To the extent that, once again, the conventions, desires, and structures of the Jamesian international tale condition Baldwin's work, they are not faithfully reproduced. Superimposing itself over *The Golden Bowl*, which in portraying the dissolution of a marriage splits in half, *Another Country* divides into three major parts, its narrative structure emerging from and commenting on the series of love triangles inscribed. I have pointed out that the novel's epigraph is taken from the preface to James's *Lady Barbarina*, in which the Master calls for a "sublime consensus of the educated." In Baldwin's hands, however, the looked-for consensus, the cultural marriage, would unite men with men, and blacks with whites. But the social systems that disable or frustrate such alliances prove to be overwhelming.

Just as James is a pronounced presence in *Another Country*, so is Hemingway, whose short story "In Another Country" is embedded in the text. But the novel undermines Hemingway's univocal masculinity. It both appropriates the textual tradition of dissent, departure, and return that Baldwin's white precursors had defined and rejects its monoculturalist underpinnings. There is a frank frustration with prior forms and a clear interest in constructing a narrative frame large enough and durable enough to accommodate race and racism, homosexual panic, and the intersections and disjunctions between homosexuality and heterosexuality, expatriation and repatriation. In *Another Country*, the meditations on exile are multiple.

If *Giovanni's Room* is hesitant about homosexual desire, *Another Country* is, by contrast, less inhibited. Baldwin's earlier novel, I have argued, implicates "The Beast in the Jungle," making homosexual panic explicit through its protagonist, David, John Marcher reimagined. The novel liberates David, but only provisionally, which perhaps accounts for contemporary gay theory's gingerly approach to it. In *Gaiety Transfigured*, for example, David Bergman argues that, taken as a whole, Baldwin's work is not specifically homosexual: "Baldwin is careful to make all his characters bisexual."[1] In fact, when I submitted a version of Chapter 4, "The Beast in *Giovanni's Room*," to a well-known progressive journal, the anonymous reader report I received could be said to summarize gay critical resistance to the text: "I think it is not a good gay politics to rescue self-oppressed types such as David; it is to gay men, not straights, that they are fatal." The problem with this particular reader's caveat is that the novel itself embarks upon a mission to rescue its central character, and in so doing attempts to uncover the cultural forces governing David's self-oppression. Gay theory may assume, or may need to assume, that those forces are no longer in place, and thus it disciplines Baldwin for eschewing sexual polemic. The impulse to dehistoricize his work, to read it as we read contemporary gay literature, is perhaps understandable; he is, after all, part of gay mythology. Baldwin mythologized falls among the figures who paved the way for homosexuality's emergence from the closet, and thus he is frequently read expectantly, hungrily. On the other hand, despite the current theoretical vogue for radical gayness, within the general culture homosexuality remains stigmatized—as stigmatized, arguably, as it was in the mid-1950s, when *Giovanni's Room* first appeared. In work after work, Baldwin suggests that homosexual self-recognition is a terrifying process in and of itself—terrifying because it involves exiling oneself from, rejecting, the social security Western culture pledges to those who obey its rules. Homosexual self-recognition potentially leads to exposure, exposure to the patriarchy's retaliation. Given the implied social risks homosexuals take when and if they do realize their sexual identities, it is hardly surprising that going on to the next step, presumably building a relationship, proves problematic. Indeed, my own supposition that a relationship is properly the next stage in the construction of a homosexual self is steeped in cultural conditioning. There *are* other possibilities.

As Teresa De Lauretis suggests in her introduction to a special issue of *Differences,*

> homosexuality is no longer to be seen simply as marginal with regard to a dominant, stable form of sexuality (heterosexuality) against which it would be defined either as merely transgressive or deviant vis-à-vis a proper, natural sexuality (i.e., institutionalized reproductive sexuality), according to the older, pathological model, or as just another optional "life-style," according to the model of contemporary North American pluralism. Instead, male and female homosexualities—in their current sexual-political articulations of gay and lesbian sexualities, in North America—may be reconceptualized as social and cultural forms in their own right, albeit emergent ones and thus still fuzzily defined, undercoded, or discursively dependent on more established forms.[2]

De Lauretis's "speculative premise" is intended to be liberating: homosexuality is not subcultural; it is countercultural. And yet it is a mistake to ignore the powerful and pervasive homophobia operating within the counterculture. A homophobia, a self-loathing, manifesting itself in, for example, the still highly visible abuse of alcohol and other drugs, suggests a controlling need to numb the senses and the mind. In my discussion of "Going to Meet the Man," I relate the text to Baldwin's "Male Prison," both an attack on Gide and an outline for a sexual manifesto that contemporary gay theory would read as "self-oppressed":

> It is possible, as it were, to have one's pleasure without paying for it. But to have one's pleasure without paying for it is precisely the way to find oneself reduced to a search for pleasure which grows steadily more desperate and more grotesque. It does not take long, after all, to discover that sex is only sex, that there are few things on earth more futile or more deadening than a meaningless round of conquests. The really horrible thing about the phenomenon of present-day homosexuality . . . is that today's unlucky *deviate* [my emphasis] can only save himself by the most tremendous exertion of all his forces from falling in to an underworld in which he never meets either men or women, where it is impossible to have either a lover or a friend, where the possibility of genuine human involvement has altogether ceased. When this possibility has ceased, so has the possibility of growth.[3]

The possibility of releasing desire (homosexual or heterosexual) from economics is not realized in *Another Country*.

Although the novel refuses to apologize for or to conceal homosexual desire, it fails to liberate the male-male relationship from its imprisonment within heterosexuality. The potentially revolutionary relationship in the text is a negotiation between men mediated by a woman. Eric, a white American actor from Alabama living in France, must decide whether his commitment to his French lover, Yves, can be sustained in America. Eric's acting career, his skill at role playing, possibly throws into relief Baldwin's position on sexual identities: they are performances. Anyone can learn how to play them. Indeed, the offer of a supporting role in a Broadway play precipitates Eric's crisis:

This offer had presented Eric with the enormous question he had spent three years avoiding. To accept it was to bring his European sojourn to an end; not to accept it was to transform his sojourn into exile. He and Yves had been together for more than two years and, from the time of their meeting, his home had been with Yves. More precisely and literally, it was Yves who had come to live with him, but each was, for the other, the dwelling place that each had despaired of finding.[4]

The anxiety articulated in this passage is unclear. If, indeed, Eric and Yves have found a "home" in each other, then why is the prospect of living in America so paralyzing? In short, does Baldwin suggest that homosexual relationships are possible only in Europe—only, that is, in another country? The figure of the homosexual in *Another Country* is the catalyst for Baldwin's attack on American culture in general. The oppression of homosexuals, in other words, is inextricably linked with the persecution of women and blacks. Europe is thus intentionally and thoroughly romanticized as *the* refuge. Which, of course, as "Stranger in the Village" demonstrates, it never was and never could be. That Eric's homosexual identity evolves in Europe both acknowledges Jamesian *Bildung* and subverts it. Assuming that, for James, America's learning from Europe would ideally result in America's embracing Europe, then Eric and Yves are exemplary. They are certainly "educated." The books in their house in France, for example, are telling: "Yves' copies of Blaise Cendrars and Jean Genet and Marcel Proust, Eric's copies of *An Actor Prepares* and *The Wings of the Dove* and *Native Son*" (195). These texts suggest a new canon, one in which traditional classifications of race, sexuality, and nationality have been dissolved.

But how is a homosexual relationship to be structured? To what existing model can it possibly look for guidance? In *Another Country* the answer is unambiguous: male-male relationships inevitably transcribe heterosexual conventions. This is not to say that the novel valorizes these conventions. Indeed, heterosexual relationships are figured as structures of repression, capitulation, and self-flagellation. Perhaps the most significant male-female relationship in the novel is an interracial one. Rufus, the black jazz musician whose suicide drives the plot forward, struggles for power and control over Leona, the southern white woman who, insofar as she represents white-liberal guilt, repeatedly submits to her lover's physical and psychological abuse—to the point that she is eventually driven to insanity. As lovers, they are at war:

> Tears hung in the corners of her eyes. . . . He wanted her to remember him the longest day she lived. And, shortly, nothing could have stopped him, not the white God himself nor a lynch mob arriving on wings. Under his breath he cursed the milk-white bitch and groaned and rode his weapon between her thighs. She began to cry. *I told you*, he moaned, *I'd give you something to cry about.* . . . A moan and a curse tore through him while he beat her with all the strength he had and felt the venom shoot out of him, enough for a hundred black-white babies. (21–22)

Cass and Richard are the embittered white bourgeois custodians of marriage. She resents her husband for his limitations as a man and, more importantly, as a writer: "Richard had bitterly disappointed her by writing a book in which he did not believe . . . [,] the book he had written to make money represented the absolute limit of his talent" (112). Richard resents Cass because he has played by the rules, worked most of his life to support his wife and two children, only to discover in middle age that the *marriage* by which he had defined himself for so long is meaningless: ". . . I've worked, I've worked very hard, Cass, for you and our children, so we could be happy and so our marriage would work" (375). Why marriages should "work," why the culture is so heavily invested in them, are the questions Cass and Richard (and, ultimately, *Another Country*) labor to answer.

In the world of the text, prescribed heterosexual gender roles, together with the power imbalances they imply, cannot be given up. Cass is not only Richard's property; she is also the property of her children. Her household is a community of men to whom she owes a heavy debt:

> Therefore, she too, was marking time, waiting—for . . . the bill to come in. Only after she had paid this bill would she really know what her resources were. And she dreaded this moment, dreaded it. . . . The terror was not merely that she did not know how she would rebuild her life, or that she feared, as she grew older, coming to despise herself: the terror was that her children would despise her. The rebuilding of her own life might have reduced itself, simply, to moving out of Richard's house—*Richard's* house! how long had she thought of it as Richard's house?—and getting a job. But holding the love of her children, and helping them to grow from boys into men—this was a different matter. (363–64)

It will become clear that Cass realizes her own authority only in drag, only within the framework of her affair with the homosexual Eric. Indeed, because all the relationships in the text are in some senses brought to trial as a result of this "bisexual" alliance, it is my ultimate focus.

That a homosexual male freely enters into a sexual relationship with a heterosexual woman would seem to shore up Bergman's position: namely, that when we read Baldwin's work in search of a pure homosexuality what we find instead is a cowardly bisexuality. It is certainly true that in *Another Country* sexual boundaries are routinely transgressed, but so are racial barriers. It is difficult to say whether the collapsing of sexual and racial binarisms reflects the novel's ideological confusion or points toward an ambitious cultural project. If, as Robert Scholes suggests, writing (reading)—an act involving seduction, violation, mastery, pleasure and pain, voyeurism, alienation—is akin to sexual intercourse,[5] then his theory of narrative may help us read *Another Country*, in which narrative discourse is represented as somatic.

Indeed, this is a novel about writing novels. Cass's sexual frustration, for example, is actualized within the context of Richard's impotence as a writer. Assuming for the moment that texts are figural bodies and that writing and reading them results from a biological urgency to reproduce, then the multiple sexual exchanges occurring in Baldwin's novel articulate what novels potentially do: they allow us to know the Other by possessing (creating) the Other. In and through texts, ideally, we penetrate foreign territories of the "flesh." And thus Vivaldo Moore, whom Richard views as both his sexual and writerly rival, is accorded considerable rhetorical authority:

> Vivaldo sat at his worktable, struggling with a chapter which was not going well. He was terribly weary—he had worked in the bookstore all day and then come downtown to do a moving job— but this was not the reason for his paralysis. He did not seem to know enough about the people in his novel. They did not seem to trust him. They were all named, more or less, all more or less destined, the pattern he wished them to describe was clear to him. But it did not seem clear to them. He could move them about but they themselves did not move. He put words in their mouths which they uttered sullenly, unconvinced. With the same agony, or greater, with which he attempted to seduce a woman, he was trying to seduce his people: he begged them to surrender up to him their privacy. (127)

Achieving a surrender of "privacy," unlocking the epistemological door barricading whiteness from blackness and heterosexuality from homosexuality, is the Baldwinian enterprise. In *Another Country* sex acts and speech acts are, in terms of their objectives, interchangeable. The men and women in the text are figures of seduction and persuasion. They invade each other, but they are finally unable to unite. Their relationships are without exception commodified, are structures of unequal exchange. The novel is a marketplace of desire, in which there are two choices: to exploit or to be exploited. Vivaldo is an insatiable consumer of blackness. Though his friendship with Rufus is not explicitly sexual, his desire for Rufus is achieved through the meditation of black women:

> In Harlem . . . he had merely dropped his load and marked the spot with silver. It had seemed much simpler for a time. But even simple pleasure, bought and paid for, did not take long to fail— pleasure, as it turned out, was not simple. When, wandering about Harlem, he came across a girl he liked, he could not fail to wish that he had met her somewhere else, under different circumstances. He could not fail to disapprove of her situation and to demand of her more than any girl in such a situation could give. If he did not like her, then he despised her and it was very painful for him to despise a colored girl, it increased his self-contempt. So that, by and by, however pressing may have been the load he carried uptown, he returned home with a greater one, not to be so easily discharged. (132)

Vivaldo's routine commodification of black women reaches its apex in the course of his affair with Ida, Rufus's sister, whom he resolves to make *his*: "She opened up before him, yet fell back before him, too, he felt that he was traveling up a savage, jungle river, looking for the source which remained hidden just beyond the black, dangerous, dripping foliage. . . . Last night she had watched him; this morning he watched her; he was determined to bring her over the edge and into his possession . . ." (177). At the end of all this, Vivaldo is the ostensible victor: "He rolled over on his back and she got out of bed and walked into the bathroom. He watched the tall, dusty body, which now belonged to him, disappear" (179). But Ida herself is acutely aware of what she has to sell and of its market value. Determined to advance her career as a singer, she has an affair with a white television producer, explaining to her "lover" Vivaldo that she had always considered white men predators:

> I used to see the way white men watched me, like dogs. And I thought about what I could do to them. How I hated them, the way they looked, and the things they'd say, all dressed up in their damn white skin, and their clothes just so, and their little weak, white pricks jumping in their drawers. You could do any damn thing with them if you just led them along, because they wanted to do something dirty and they knew that you knew how. All black people knew that. Only, the polite ones didn't say dirty. They said real. I used to wonder what in the world they did in bed, white people I mean, between themselves, to get them so sick. . . . I didn't want their little change, I didn't want to be at their mercy. I wanted them to be at mine. (418–19)

I have said that Eric's relationship with Yves is potentially revolutionary. It is the focus of book two—exactly in the center of the narrative. But one begins to wonder whether the relationship under construction is in translation. Blackness, in short, as I have argued of *Giovanni's Room*, has been transmuted into whiteness. At the beginning of what is essentially their book, Eric and Yves cavort in their garden, situated somewhere in the south of France. But the reproduced Jamesian European scene is one in which blackness is implicit from the start: "Yves' tiny black-and-white kitten stalked the garden as though it were Africa, crouching beneath the mimosas like a panther and leaping into the air" (183). Taken as a whole, the novel is as two-toned as the kitten, straddling black and white textual traditions, conflating black and white bodies. James, in other words, is not the only authoritative voice in the text. There is the authority of the blues in general, and of W. C. Handy and Bessie Smith in particular. And of course, as Eric's book collection attests, Richard Wright can be heard as well.

Eric is drawn to Yves because he reminds him of Rufus, at one time Eric's sadistic lover. Desire, once again, is triangular. Further, Eric's "love" for Yves is defined in terms of retributive power. As Eric had suffered, so must Yves. Rufus, we are told, "had made Eric pay for such pleasure as Eric gave, or got. . . . He had despised Eric's manhood by treating him as a woman, by telling him how inferior he was to a woman, by treating him as nothing more than a hideous sexual deformity" (46). But the torture Rufus inflicts on his male lover is a response to Eric's equally indefensible racism: "Rufus' great power over him had to do with the past which Eric had buried in some deep, dark place; was connected with himself, in Alabama, . . . with the cold white people and the warm, black people, warm at least for him, and as necessary as the sun . . ." (193–94).

The values Eric assigns to blackness are glaringly essentialist: blackness is a force of nature—"necessary" because it soothes the troubled white soul. Eric is captivated by the entire black race: "Was it the body of Rufus to which he had clung, or the bodies of dark men, seen briefly, somewhere, in a garden or a clearing, long ago, sweat running down their chocolate chests and shoulders, their voices ringing out, the white of their jock-straps beautiful against their skin, one with his head tilted back before a dipper—and the water splashing, sparkling, singing down!—one with his arm raised, laying an axe to the base of a tree?" (194). As a child "[h]e had loved the cook, a black woman named Grace, who fed him and spanked him and scolded and coddled him, and dried the tears which scarcely anyone else in the household ever saw. But, even more than he had loved Grace, he had loved her husband, Henry" (197). Henry, in fact, is for Eric literally a love object:

> He had thrown himself into Henry's arms, almost sobbing himself, and yet somehow wise enough to hold his own tears back. He was filled with an unutterably painful rage against whatever it was that

had hurt Henry. It was the first time he had felt a man's arms around him, the first time he had felt the chest and belly of a man; he had been ten or eleven years old. He had been terribly frightened, obscurely and profoundly frightened, but he had not, as the years were to prove, been frightened enough. He knew that what he felt was somehow wrong, and must be kept a secret; but he thought that it was wrong because Henry was a grown man, and colored, and he was a little boy, and white. (198)

As an adolescent, Eric was in love with "a colored boy. His name was LeRoy, he was seventeen, a year older than Eric, and he worked as a porter in the courthouse. He was tall and very black, and taciturn" (201). The relationship permits Eric's first unambiguous homosexual experience:

That day. That day. Had he known where that day would lead him would he have writhed as he did, in such an anguished joy, beneath the great weight of his first lover? But if he had known, or been capable of caring, where such a day might lead him, it could never have been his necessity to bring about such a day. He was frightened and in pain and the boy who held him so relentlessly was suddenly a stranger; and yet this stranger worked in Eric an eternal, a healing transformation. (206)

Exploiting his power, Eric realizes himself as a homosexual at the expense of others. His wholly self-interested love for the hired man Henry and his wife, Grace, leads to their dismissal from the household: "Henry and Grace were eventually banished, due to some lapse or offense on Henry's part. Since Eric's parents had never approved of those sessions in the furnace room, Eric always suspected this as the reason for Henry's banishment, which made his opposition to his parents more bitter than ever" (198). In his determination to possess LeRoy, Eric minimizes the social risk his lover takes each time they meet: "You a nice boy, Eric, but you don't know the score. Your Daddy *owns* half the folks in this town, ain't but so much they can do to you. But what they can do to *me*—!" (205–6).

Even Eric's relationship with Yves, predictably, is as commodified as any other in the text. Senior to Yves both in age and experience, Eric is cast in the role of protector and provider. Indeed, the novel is unable to determine whether a relationship between men can be conducted differently. The house on the Mediterranean is Eric's, as is the money; in exchange, Yves trades his body. Moreover, the arrangement, the contract, is not binding but is instead designed to be broken: "On the day that Yves no longer needed him, Eric would drop back into chaos" (210). Discursively, their desire for each other is work:

> They labored together slowly, violently, a long time: both feared the end. Both feared the morning, when the moon and stars would be gone, when this room would be harsh and sorrowful with sunlight, and this bed would be dismantled, waiting for other flesh. *Love is expensive,* Yves had once said, with his curiously dry wonder. *One must put furniture around it, or it goes.* Now, for a while, there would be no furniture—how long would this night have to last them? What would the morning bring? the imminent morning, behind which were hidden so many mornings, so many nights. (225–26)

What becomes clear in *Another Country* is that rescuing human relationships from the sexual marketplace is not a choice available to us in a postmodern world. Yves maintains, for example, that everyone is a prostitute. He refers to his mother as a *putain*. And of women in general he says: "I do not like *l'élégance des femmes.* Every time I see a woman wearing her fur coats and her jewels and her gowns, I want to tear all that off her and drag her someplace, to a *pissoir,* and make her smell the smell of many men, the *piss* of many men, and make her know that *that* is what she is for, she is no better than that, she does not fool me with all those shining rags, which, anyway, she only got by blackmailing some

stupid man" (210). This misogyny is not foregrounded as homosexual, but as heterosexual. The values Yves assigns to women are
those of the patriarchy.

As I have suggested, whether Eric's relationship with Yves can
survive when transplanted in American soil is among the novel's
organizing questions. And yet, almost immediately upon Eric's
arrival in New York (Yves postpones his pilgrimage across the
Atlantic, deferring to his lover), he plunges into an affair with a
woman—with Cass, who denies that her affair with Eric reproduces the love she had once felt for her husband, Richard: "I don't
know what's going to happen between Richard and me," she tells
Eric. "But it isn't *you* that's come between Richard and me—*you*
don't have anything to do with that" (287). When, of course, in a
novel in which desire is always mediated, Eric has everything to
do with it. Cass, we are told, essentially has two choices: to return
to her marriage or to resign herself to paying for sex for the rest
of her life.

> She was frightened because she had never before found herself play-
> ing so anomalous a role and because nothing in her experience had
> ever suggested that her body could become a trap for boys, and the
> tomb of her self-esteem. She had embarked on a voyage which might
> end years from now in some horrible villa, near a blue sea, with some
> unspeaking, unspeakably phallic, Turk or Spaniard or Jew or Greek
> or Arabian. Yet, she did not want it to stop. (287–88)

If Cass's relationship with Eric is potentially the first in a series
of humiliating sexual exchanges, what does his involvement with
Cass anticipate? At the start of their affair, Eric says: "I know we
have *now*, but I don't think we have much of a future" (287). He
is an actor, accustomed to role playing; yet, on the other hand,
why attempt such a performance when, as he informs Cass,
"[Yves] *is* coming, and we *have* been together for over two years.
And that means something" (289)—when, in short, Eric has found

a man who not only wants to live with him but who also loves him? I would suggest—and this is why gay theorists have read the novel skeptically—that *Another Country*, like *Giovanni's Room*, is unable to affirm the legitimacy of homosexual relationships. Its anxiety in this regard emerges from Freudian homosexual paradigms that even at this comparatively late point within the trajectory of Baldwin's career continue to frustrate the male-male relationship. To Eric's revelation that "[Yves] hates his mother, or thinks he does" (289), Cass replies: "That's not the usual pattern, is it? . . . I mean, from what we're told, most men with a sexual bias toward men love their mothers and hate their fathers" (289). Eric rejects the theory, insisting that "we haven't been told much" (289), but the novel as a whole possibly does not. The perspective on Eric's sexual development is blurred: ". . . he lived his life . . . at school by day and before his mirror by night, dressed up in his mother's old clothes or in whatever colorful scraps he had been able to collect, posturing and, in a whisper, declaiming" (198–99). Is this homosexual self-recognition (". . . lesbians and gay men often contour their oppositional identities through appropriations of the very stereotypes through which each group is represented within the political imaginary of hetero-patriarchy")?[6] Or is it, on Freud's terms, a pathology: a clear case of arrested development?

Further, what may befall Cass without Richard is postulated as Eric's inevitable fate without Yves:

> He remembered that army of lonely men who had used him, who had wrestled with him, caressed him, and submitted to him, in a darkness deeper than the darkest night. It was not merely his body they had used, but something else; his infirmity had made him the receptacle of an anguish which he could scarcely believe was in the world. (210–11)

Eric's unconventional maleness and Cass's conventional womanhood are reflexive: both desire men and both have been victimized by men. If within the narrative design Eric is a metaphorical exploited woman, then his relationship with Cass is potentially an equal partnership, a "female" alliance.

Nevertheless, as a narrative event, their "love affair" is overdetermined—at once explicitly heterosexual, implicitly homosexual, and suggestively incestuous. Viewing Eric's naked body for the first time, Cass thinks of "her children, Paul and Michael, which had come, so miraculously formed, and so heavy and secret with promise, out of her" (291). As lovers, then, Cass and Eric are mother and son: "He took her like a boy, with that singlemindedness, and with a boy's passion to please. . . . Eventually, he slept on her breast, like a child" (291–92). But beyond this, there is a reversal of traditional heterosexual roles. With Eric, Cass is not submissive: she is served. Her husband, Richard, assumes that she must have deferred to Eric ("Did he fuck you in the ass, did he make you suck his cock? Answer me, you bitch, you slut, you *cunt!*" [376]), but this assumption comments on Richard's understanding of sex as an act of power and control. Indeed, forcing his wife to confess the details, he beats her: "He pulled her head forward, then slammed it back against the chair, and slapped her across the face, twice, as hard as he could" (375–76). But Richard's abusive behavior is motivated by more than betrayal; it is also deeply rooted in his anxiety about his authority as a man. Richard considers Eric a woman, which in his eyes makes Cass a powerful threat. The subtext for this scene is an earlier conversation. Richard: "What a funny girl you are. . . . You've got a bad case of penis envy." Cass: "So do most men" (108).

One might say that in *Another Country* "penis envy" is pervasive. Yet the novel abhors its own phallocentrism, and thus it anticipates "Going to Meet the Man," the narrative with which I began. Sexism will cease, in short, when racism ceases. Homosexuals will be liberated when heterosexuals are liberated. But only in another country—which is to say in another (a different), an inarticulable world.[7]

NOTES

Introduction

1. Henry Louis Gates, Jr., "Criticism in the Jungle," in *Black Literature and Literary Theory*, ed. Henry Louis Gates, Jr. (New York: Methuen, 1984), 3.

2. See Toni Morrison, *Playing in the Dark: Whiteness and the Literary Imagination* (Cambridge: Harvard University Press, 1992).

3. C. W. E. Bigsby, "The Second Black Renaissance," in *The Second Black Renaissance: Essays in Black Literature*, Contributions in Afro-American and African Studies 50, ed. Hollis R. Lynch (Westport, Conn.: Greenwood Press, 1980), 29.

4. Edward Said, *The World, the Text, and the Critic* (Cambridge: Harvard University Press, 1983), 17.

5. See my discussion of James's injunction in Chapter 6.

6. Bigsby, "The Second Black Renaissance," 26.

7. Ibid., 29.

8. Malcolm Cowley, *Exile's Return: A Literary Odyssey of the 1920s* (1934, 1956; reprint, New York: Penguin, 1976), 242.

9. Ibid., 243.

10. Humphrey Carpenter, *Geniuses Together: American Writers in Paris in the 1920s* (Boston: Houghton, 1988), ix.

11. Ibid., 16.

12. Wallace Martin, *Recent Theories of Narrative* (Ithaca: Cornell University Press, 1986), 44.

13. Ernest Earnest, *Expatriates and Patriots: American Artists, Scholars, and Writers in Europe* (Durham: Duke University Press, 1968), 280. Others appear to endorse this view. See, for example, Jerome Klinkowitz, *The*

New American Novel: The Fiction of Richard Yates, Dan Wakefield, and Thomas McGuane (Athens: University of Georgia Press, 1986), 60. Klinkowitz argues that "James was the last major American novelist of manners who felt compelled to take up residence abroad in order to find a world suitable to his descriptive talents."

14. Samuel Putnam, *Paris Was Our Mistress: Memoirs of a Lost and Found Generation* (New York: Viking, 1947), 63.

15. Harold Cruse, *The Crisis of the Negro Intellectual* (New York: William Morrow, 1967), 465.

16. F. Scott Fitzgerald, *The Crack-Up*, ed. Edmund Wilson (1945; reprint, New York: Scribner's, 1956), 73. Subsequent page references are to this edition.

17. I refer, of course, to Sontag's essay "Notes on 'Camp,' " in *Against Interpretation* (New York: Dell, 1966).

18. Houston A. Baker, Jr., *Modernism and the Harlem Renaissance* (Chicago: University of Chicago Press, 1987), 6.

19. Toril Moi, *Sexual/Textual Politics: Feminist Literary Theory* (London: Methuen, 1985), xiv.

20. The concluding phrase of this sentence alludes to Said's argument on *Madame Bovary* in *The World, the Text, and the Critic,* 117. He observes that Emma's "desire to live romantically . . . is at once her distinction and affliction."

Chapter 1

1. Henry James, *Hawthorne* (1879; reprint, Ithaca: Cornell University Press, 1956), 34.

2. James Baldwin, "Stranger in the Village," in *The Price of the Ticket: Collected Nonfiction, 1948–1985* (New York: St. Martin's, 1985), 79.

3. James Baldwin, "The Discovery of What It Means to Be an American," in *The Price of the Ticket,* 171.

4. Henry James, *The Art of the Novel,* ed. R. P. Blackmur (New York: Scribner's, 1934), 209.

5. Ian F. A. Bell, introduction to *Henry James: Fiction as History,* ed. Ian F. A. Bell (London: Vision, 1984), 7.

6. Henry James, *The American Scene,* ed. Leon Edel (1907; Bloomington: Indiana University Press, 1968), 121.

7. W. J. Weatherby, *James Baldwin: Artist on Fire* (New York: Dell, 1989), 96.

8. Baldwin, "Discovery," 171.

9. Charles Newman, "The Lesson of the Master: Henry James and James Baldwin," *Yale Review* 56 (October 1966): 45–46.

10. Horace Porter, *Stealing the Fire: The Art and Protest of James Baldwin* (Middletown, Conn.: Wesleyan University Press, 1989), 125–53.

11. Quoted in Weatherby, *James Baldwin*, 97.

12. Toni Morrison, *Playing in the Dark: Whiteness and the Literary Imagination* (Cambridge: Harvard University Press, 1992), 4.

13. Ibid., 4.

14. Ibid., 13–14.

15. Wendy Steiner, "Review of *Playing in the Dark*," *New York Times Book Review* (5 April 1992), 9.

16. James Baldwin, "Going to Meet the Man," in *Going to Meet the Man* (New York: Dial, 1965), 229. Subsequent page references are to this edition.

17. James Baldwin, "The Male Prison," in *The Price of the Ticket*, 101–2.

18. Baldwin, "Stranger," 88.

19. Cornel West, *Race Matters* (Boston: Beacon, 1993), 83–84.

20. Joel Kovel, *White Racism: A Psychohistory* (New York: Random, 1970), 67.

21. Ibid.

22. Ibid.

23. David Adams Leeming, "An Interview with James Baldwin on Henry James," *Henry James Review* 8 (Fall 1986): 49.

24. Ibid.

Chapter 2

1. F. Scott Fitzgerald, *The Great Gatsby* (1925; reprint, New York: Scribner's, 1953), 13. Subsequent page references are to this edition.

2. Nina Auerbach, *Communities of Women: An Idea in Fiction* (Cambridge: Harvard University Press, 1978), 122.

3. Ibid., 116.

4. William Wasserstrom, *Heiress of All the Ages* (Minneapolis: University of Minnesota Press, 1959), ix.

5. Ibid., x.

6. F. W. Dupee, *Henry James* (1951; reprint, New York: William Morrow, 1974), 110–11.

7. Wasserstrom, *Heiress of All the Ages*, 63.

8. Bakhtin argues that discourse in the novel straddles two stylistic lines. Novels of the first type "eliminate their brute heteroglossia [the competing linguistic forces derived from everyday speech that Bakhtin maintains are unique to the novel], replacing it everywhere with a single-imaged, 'ennobled' language." Novels of this category, then, homogenize difference. Novels of the second type, however, incorporate a multiplicity of "languages, manners, genres; . . . [they] force all exhausted and used-up, all socially and ideologically alien and distant worlds to speak for themselves in their own language and in their own style. . . ." M. M. Bakhtin, *The Dialogic Imagination*, ed. Michael Holquist, trans. Caryl Emerson and Michael Holquist (Austin: University of Texas Press, 1981), 409–10.

And yet, just as the author's intentions are dialogically linked with these languages, they are also dialogically opposed to them, thereby energizing the text with unresolved conflict. The two styles of novelistic discourse Bakhtin identifies are sometimes present within the same text, and so the reader must contend not only with heteroglossia but also with oppositional modes of discourse. Such is the case with *Daisy Miller*. Bakhtinian theory, of course, assumes a democratic reader.

9. Wasserstrom, *Heiress of All the Ages*, x.

10. Ibid., 65.

11. Henry James, *Daisy Miller*, in *Selected Fiction*, ed. Leon Edel (New York: Dutton, 1964), 61–62. Subsequent page references are to this edition.

12. Richard Godden, "Some Slight Shifts in the Manner of the Novel of Manners," in *Henry James: Fiction as History*, ed. Ian F. A. Bell (London: Vision, 1984), 162.

13. Ibid.

14. Ibid., 168.

15. Houston A. Baker, Jr., *Modernism and the Harlem Renaissance* (Chicago: University of Chicago Press, 1987), 6.

16. Ibid., 4.

17. T. S. Eliot, "Notes on 'The Waste Land,' " in *The Complete Poems and Plays: 1909–1950* (New York: Harcourt, 1971), 152.

18. René Girard, *Violence and the Sacred*, trans. Patrick Gregory (Baltimore: Johns Hopkins University Press, 1977), 95.

19. Henry James, *The American Scene*, ed. Leon Edel (1907; Bloomington: Indiana University Press, 1968), 102.

20. Virginia Fowler, *Henry James's American Girl: The Embroidery on the Canvas* (Madison: University of Wisconsin Press, 1984), 16.

21. See Theodor W. Adorno, "Jazz," in *Prisms*, trans. Samuel and Shierry Weber (1967; Cambridge: MIT Press, 1984), 121–32.

22. Matthew J. Bruccoli, introduction to *New Essays on "The Great Gatsby,"* ed. Matthew J. Bruccoli, The American Novel 2 (Cambridge: Cambridge University Press, 1985), 7.

23. James, *The American Scene*, 212.

24. Joan Didion, *Slouching towards Bethlehem* (1968; reprint, New York: Touchstone, 1979), 211–12.

25. Lionel Trilling, *The Liberal Imagination* (New York: Viking, 1950), 244.

26. F. Scott Fitzgerald, *Tender Is the Night* (1934; reprint, New York: Scribner's, 1962), 9. Subsequent page references are to this edition.

Chapter 3

1. F. Scott Fitzgerald, *Tender Is the Night* (1934; reprint, New York: Scribner's, 1962), 134. Subsequent page reference is to this edition.

2. F. Scott Fitzgerald, *The Great Gatsby* (1925; reprint, New York: Scribner's, 1953), 97. Subsequent page references are to this edition.

3. See Philip Fisher, *Hard Facts* (New York: Oxford University Press, 1987), 3–21.

4. Jan Nederveen Pieterse, *White on Black: Images of Africa and Blacks in Western Popular Culture* (New Haven: Yale University Press, 1992), 10.

5. André Le Vot, *F. Scott Fitzgerald*, trans. William Byron (New York: Doubleday, 1983), xi.

6. Whether Fitzgerald had actually read Spengler is impossible to say—though his letters suggest that he had. See in particular his remarks (6 June 1940) to Maxwell Perkins, in which he asks: "Did you ever read

Spengler—specifically including the second volume? I read him the same summer I was writing *The Great Gatsby* and I don't think I ever quite recovered from him" (*The Letters*, ed. Andrew Turnbull [New York: Scribner's, 1963], 289–90). Of course, *The Decline of the West* had not yet been published in English in the summer of 1924. The point, however, is that Fitzgerald had attended to Spengler's ideas, even though he may have relied on the reports of others.

7. John F. Callahan, *The Illusions of a Nation: Myth and History in the Novels of F. Scott Fitzgerald* (Urbana: University of Illinois Press, 1972), 92.

8. F. Scott Fitzgerald, *The Crack-Up*, ed. Edmund Wilson (1945; reprint, New York: Scribner's, 1956), 78.

9. Callahan, *The Illusions of a Nation*, 93.

10. Ibid.

11. Harriet Beecher Stowe, *Uncle Tom's Cabin* (1852; reprint, Toronto: Bantam, 1981), 248.

12. Jane Tompkins, *Sensational Designs: The Cultural Work of American Fiction, 1790–1860* (New York: Oxford University Press, 1985), 131.

13. Ibid., 141.

14. Michel Fabre, *La Rive Noire: De Harlem à la Seine* (Paris: Lieu Commun, 1985), 12.

15. Edwin Fussell, "Fitzgerald's Brave New World," *Critical Essays on "Tender Is the Night,"* ed. Milton R. Stern, Critical Essays on American Literature (Boston: G. K. Hall, 1986), 116.

16. Callahan, *The Illusions of a Nation*, 132–33.

17. Ibid., 131.

18. Fitzgerald, *The Letters*, 326.

19. Malcolm Cowley, introduction to *Tender Is the Night*, by F. Scott Fitzgerald (New York: Scribner's, 1951), xv.

Chapter 4

1. Henry Louis Gates, Jr., "'Authenticity,' or the Lesson of Little Tree," *New York Times Book Review* (24 November 1991), 28.

2. Robert A. Bone, "The Novels of James Baldwin," in *Images of the Negro in American Literature*, ed. Seymour L. Gross and John E. Hardy (Chicago: University of Chicago Press, 1966), 283.

3. Eve Kosofsky Sedgwick, "The Beast in the Closet: James and the Writing of Homosexual Panic," in *Epistemology of the Closet* (Berkeley and Los Angeles: University of California Press, 1990), 197.

4. Claude J. Summers, *Gay Fictions, Wilde to Stonewall: Studies in a Male Homosexual Literary Tradition* (New York: Continuum, 1990), 173.

5. James Baldwin, *Giovanni's Room* (New York: Dial, 1956), 3. Subsequent page references are to this edition.

6. James Baldwin, "Alas, Poor Richard," in *The Price of the Ticket: Collected Nonfiction, 1948–1985* (New York: St. Martin's, 1985), 279.

7. Eldridge Cleaver, *Soul on Ice* (New York: Dell, 1968), 106.

8. Richard Wright, *Native Son* (1940; reprint, New York: Harper, 1987), xxvii.

9. See Horace Porter, *Stealing the Fire: The Art and Protest of James Baldwin* (Middletown, Conn.: Wesleyan University Press, 1989), 142–46.

10. Cleaver, *Soul on Ice*, 105.

11. David Bergman, *Gaiety Transfigured: Gay Self-Representation in American Literature* (Madison: University of Wisconsin Press, 1991), 168.

12. Richard Goldstein, " 'Go the Way Your Blood Beats': An Interview with James Baldwin," *Village Voice* (26 June 1984), 13. Subsequent page references are to this issue.

13. Henry James, "The Beast in the Jungle," in *Selected Fiction*, ed. Leon Edel (New York: Dutton, 1964), 536. Subsequent page references are to this edition.

14. Eve Kosofsky Sedgwick, *Between Men: English Literature and Male Homosocial Desire* (New York: Columbia University Press, 1985), 25.

15. Sedgwick, *Epistemology of the Closet*, 207.

16. Joseph Allen Boone, *Tradition counter Tradition: Love and the Form of Fiction* (Chicago: University of Chicago Press, 1987), 191.

17. Sedgwick, *Epistemology of the Closet*, 210–11.

Chapter 5

1. Addison Gayle, "The Function of Black Literature at the Present Time," in *The Black Aesthetic*, ed. Addison Gayle (New York: Doubleday, 1971), 413.

2. Harold Cruse, *The Crisis of the Negro Intellectual* (New York: William Morrow, 1967), 413.

3. Ibid., 482.

4. Eldridge Cleaver, *Soul on Ice* (New York: Dell, 1968), 102.

5. Ibid., 100.

6. Henry Louis Gates, Jr., "Tell Me, Sir . . . What *Is* Black Literature?" special issue of *PMLA* 105.1 (January 1990): 11–22.

7. Quoted ibid., 11.

8. Quoted ibid., 20.

9. F. Scott Fitzgerald, *Tender Is the Night* (1934; reprint, New York: Scribner's, 1962), 151.

10. James Baldwin, "Stranger in the Village," in *The Price of the Ticket: Collected Nonfiction, 1948–1985* (New York: St. Martin's, 1985), 79. Subsequent page references are to this edition.

11. Henry Louis Gates, Jr., "Authority, (White) Power, and the (Black) Critic," special issue of *Cultural Critique* 7 (Fall 1987): 45.

12. Ibid., 35.

13. Gayle, "Function of Black Literature," 414.

14. Marianna Torgovnick, *Gone Primitive: Savage Intellects, Modern Lives* (Chicago: University of Chicago Press, 1990), 8–9.

Chapter 6

1. James Baldwin, "The Discovery of What It Means to Be an American," in *The Price of the Ticket: Collected Nonfiction, 1948–1985* (New York: St. Martin's, 1985), 175.

2. William Boelhower, "Avant-Garde Autobiography: Deconstructing the Modernist Habitat," typescript, Department of Afro-American Studies, Harvard University, 20.

3. Ibid., 4.

4. Henry James, *The American Scene,* ed. Leon Edel (1907; Bloomington: Indiana University Press, 1968), 101. Subsequent page references are to this edition.

5. Henry James to William James, 29 October 1889, *The Letters,* ed. Percy Lubbock (New York: Scribner's, 1920).

6. Leon Edel, introduction to *The American Scene,* by Henry James, xvi.

7. Arnold Rampersad, "Slavery and the Literary Imagination: Du

Bois's *The Souls of Black Folk*," in *Slavery and the Literary Imagination*, ed. Deborah E. McDowell and Arnold Rampersad (Baltimore: Johns Hopkins University Press, 1989), 105.

8. W. E. B. Du Bois, *The Souls of Black Folk*, ed. J. Saunders Redding (1903; New York: Fawcett, 1961), 231.

9. Edel, introduction to *The American Scene*, by Henry James, xxii.

10. Ibid., xxiv.

11. David Levering Lewis, *When Harlem Was in Vogue* (New York: Knopf, 1981), 27.

12. Cited in Caroline Golab, *Immigrant Destinations* (Philadelphia: Temple University Press, 1977), 19.

13. Myra Jehlen, "Gender," in *Critical Terms for Literary Study*, ed. Frank Lentricchia and Thomas McLaughlin (Chicago: University of Chicago Press, 1990), 273.

14. See William Boelhower, *Through a Glass Darkly* (New York: Oxford University Press, 1987), 26–28.

15. Edith Wharton, *The House of Mirth*, ed. Elizabeth Ammons (1905; New York: Norton, 1990), 13, 16.

16. Philip Fisher, *Hard Facts* (New York: Oxford University Press, 1987), 3–21.

17. Eve Kosofsky Sedgwick, *Epistemology of the Closet* (Berkeley and Los Angeles: University of California Press, 1990), 197.

18. Ibid.

19. James Baldwin, "Fifth Avenue, Uptown," in *The Price of the Ticket*, 205. Subsequent page references are to this edition.

20. James Baldwin, "East River, Downtown," in *The Price of the Ticket*, 266. Subsequent page references are to this edition.

21. Barbara Johnson, *A World of Difference* (Baltimore: Johns Hopkins University Press, 1987), 173.

22. Ibid., 177.

23. Ibid., 173.

Chapter 7

1. David Bergman, *Gaiety Transfigured: Gay Self-Representation in American Literature* (Madison: University of Wisconsin Press, 1991), 165.

2. Teresa De Lauretis, "Queer Theory: Lesbian and Gay Sexualities," special issue of *Differences* 3 (Summer 1991): iii.

3. James Baldwin, "The Male Prison," in *The Price of the Ticket: Collected Nonfiction, 1948–1985* (New York: St. Martin's, 1985), 104.

4. James Baldwin, *Another Country* (New York: Dial, 1962), 184. Subsequent page references are to this edition.

5. See Robert Scholes, *Fabulation and Metafiction* (Urbana: University of Illinois Press, 1979).

6. Earl Jackson, Jr., "Scandalous Subjects: Robert Gluck's Embodied Narratives," special issue of *Differences* 3 (Summer 1991): 115.

7. I am alluding to Baldwin's epigraph, which as I have noted is taken from James's preface to *Lady Barbarina*. The epigraph is quoted in full in Chapter 1.

SELECT BIBLIOGRAPHY

Adorno, Theodor W. "Jazz." In *Prisms*. Trans. Samuel and Shierry Weber. 1967. Cambridge: MIT Press, 1984.

Aldridge, John W. *After the Lost Generation*. New York: Noonday Press, 1958.

Arlen, Michael J. *Exiles*. New York: Farrar, 1970.

Auerbach, Nina. *Communities of Women: An Idea in Fiction*. Cambridge: Harvard University Press, 1978.

Baker, Houston A., Jr. *Modernism and the Harlem Renaissance*. Chicago: University of Chicago Press, 1987.

Baker, Houston A., Jr., and Patricia Redmond, eds. *Afro-American Literary Study in the 1990s*. Chicago: University of Chicago Press, 1989.

Baker, Paul R. *The Fortunate Pilgrims: Americans in Italy, 1800–1860*. Cambridge: Harvard University Press, 1964.

Bakhtin, M. M. *The Dialogic Imagination*. Ed. Michael Holquist. Trans. Caryl Emerson and Michael Holquist. Austin: University of Texas Press, 1981.

Baldwin, James. *Another Country*. New York: Dial, 1962.

———. *Giovanni's Room*. New York: Dial, 1956.

———. "Going to Meet the Man." In *Going to Meet the Man*. New York: Dial, 1965.

———. *The Price of the Ticket: Collected Nonfiction, 1948–1985*. New York: St. Martin's, 1985.

Bell, Ian F. A. Introduction to *Henry James: Fiction as History*. Ed. Ian F. A. Bell. London: Vision, 1984.

Benstock, Shari. *Women of the Left Bank: Paris, 1900–1940.* Austin: University of Texas Press, 1986.

Bercovitch, Sacvan, and Myra Jehlen, eds. *Ideology and Classic American Literature.* Cambridge: Cambridge University Press, 1986.

Bergman, David. *Gaiety Transfigured: Gay Self-Representation in American Literature.* Madison: University of Wisconsin Press, 1991.

Bigsby, C. W. E. "The Divided Mind of James Baldwin." In *The Second Black Renaissance: Essays in Black Literature.* Contributions in Afro-American and African Studies 50. Ed. Hollis R. Lynch. Westport, Conn.: Greenwood Press, 1980.

———. "Europe, America, and the Cultural Debate." In *Superculture: American Popular Culture and Europe.* Ed. C. W. E. Bigsby. London: Paul Elek, 1975.

Blackmur, R. P. "The American Literary Expatriate." In *Foreign Influences in American Life: Essays and Critical Biographies.* Ed. David F. Bowers. Princeton: Princeton University Press, 1944.

Boelhower, William. "Avant-Garde Autobiography: Deconstructing the Modernist Habitat." Typescript. Department of Afro-American Studies, Harvard University.

———. *Through a Glass Darkly.* New York: Oxford University Press, 1987.

Bone, Robert A. "The Novels of James Baldwin." In *Images of the Negro in American Literature.* Ed. Seymour L. Gross and John E. Hardy. Chicago: University of Chicago Press, 1966.

Boone, Joseph Allen. *Tradition counter Tradition: Love and the Form of Fiction.* Chicago: University of Chicago Press, 1987.

———, ed. *Engendering Men: The Question of Male Feminist Criticism.* New York: Routledge, 1990.

Boorstin, Daniel J. *America and the Image of Europe: Reflections on American Thought.* New York: Meridian, 1960.

———. *The Americans: The National Experience.* New York: Random, 1965.

Bourdieu, Pierre. *Distinction: A Social Critique of the Judgement of Taste.* Trans. Richard Nice. Cambridge: Harvard University Press, 1984.

Bradbury, Malcolm. *The Expatriate Tradition in American Literature.* Durham: British Association for American Studies, 1982.

Broe, Mary Lynn, and Angela Ingram, eds. *Women's Writing in Exile.* Chapel Hill: University of North Carolina Press, 1989.

Browning, Frank. *The Culture of Desire: Paradox and Perversity in Gay Lives Today.* New York: Crown, 1993.

Bruccoli, Matthew J. Introduction to *New Essays on "The Great Gatsby."* Ed. Matthew J. Bruccoli. The American Novel 2. Cambridge: Cambridge University Press, 1985.

Callaghan, Morley. *That Summer in Paris.* New York: Penguin, 1979.

Callahan, John F. *The Illusions of a Nation: Myth and History in the Novels of F. Scott Fitzgerald.* Urbana: University of Illinois Press, 1972.

Campbell, James. *Talking at the Gates: A Life of James Baldwin.* New York: Penguin, 1991.

Carpenter, Humphrey. *Geniuses Together: American Writers in Paris in the 1920s.* Boston: Houghton, 1988.

Cleaver, Eldridge. *Soul on Ice.* New York: Dell, 1968.

Cliff, Michelle. *The Land of Look Behind.* New York: Firebrand, 1985.

Cowley, Malcolm. *Exile's Return: A Literary Odyssey of the 1920s.* 1934; 1956. Reprint. New York: Penguin, 1976.

————. Introduction to *Tender Is the Night,* by F. Scott Fitzgerald. New York: Scribner's, 1951.

Craige, Betty Jean, ed. *Literature, Language, and Politics.* Athens: University of Georgia Press, 1988.

Crew, Louie, ed. *The Gay Academic.* Palm Springs, Calif.: ETC, 1978.

Cruse, Harold. *The Crisis of the Negro Intellectual.* New York: William Morrow, 1967.

Davis, Ursula Broschke. *Paris without Regret: James Baldwin, Kenny Clarke, Chester Himes, and Donald Byrd.* Iowa City: University of Iowa Press, 1986.

Dearborn, Mary V. *Pocahontas's Daughters: Gender and Ethnicity in American Culture.* Chapel Hill: University of North Carolina Press, 1986.

De Lauretis, Teresa. "Queer Theory: Lesbian and Gay Sexualities." Special issue of *Differences* 3 (Summer 1991).

Denny, Margaret, and William H. Gilman. *The American Writer and the European Experience.* Minneapolis: University of Minnesota Press, 1950.

Didion, Joan. *Slouching towards Bethlehem.* 1968. Reprint. New York: Touchstone, 1979.

Du Bois, W. E. B. *The Souls of Black Folk.* 1903. Ed. J. Saunders Redding. New York: Fawcett, 1961.

Dunbar, Ernest. *The Black Expatriates: A Study of American Negroes in Exile.* New York: Dutton, 1968.

Dupee, F. W. *Henry James.* 1951. Reprint. New York: William Morrow, 1974.

Earnest, Ernest. *Expatriates and Patriots: American Artists, Scholars, and Writers in Europe.* Durham: Duke University Press, 1968.

————. *The Single Vision: The Alienation of American Intellectuals.* New York: New York University Press, 1970.

Eckman, Fern Marja. *The Furious Passage of James Baldwin.* New York: Evans, 1966.

Edel, Leon. *The Life of Henry James.* 5 vols. New York: Avon, 1978.

Fabre, Michel. *La Rive Noire: De Harlem à la Seine.* Paris: Lieu Commun, 1985.

Fetterly, Judith. *The Resisting Reader: A Feminist Approach to American Fiction.* Bloomington: Indiana University Press, 1978.

Fiedler, Leslie. *An End to Innocence: Essays on Culture and Politics.* Boston: Beacon, 1955.

Fisher, Philip. *Hard Facts.* New York: Oxford University Press, 1987.

Fishman, Solomon. *The Disinherited of Art: Writer and Background.* Berkeley and Los Angeles: University of California Press, 1953.

Fitch, Noel Riley. *Sylvia Beach and the Lost Generation: A History of Literary Paris in the Twenties and Thirties.* New York: Norton, 1983.

Fitzgerald, F. Scott. *The Crack-Up.* 1945. Ed. Edmund Wilson. Reprint. New York: Scribner's, 1956.

————. *The Great Gatsby.* 1925. Reprint. New York: Scribner's, 1953.

————. "The Hotel Child." In *Bits of Paradise: Twenty-One Uncollected Stories by F. Scott and Zelda Fitzgerald.* Ed. Matthew Bruccoli. London: Bodley Head, 1973.

————. *The Letters.* Ed. Andrew Turnbull. New York: Scribner's, 1963.

————. *Tender Is the Night.* 1934. Reprint. New York: Scribner's, 1962.

Flanner, Janet. *Paris Was Yesterday.* New York: Viking, 1972.

Fowler, Virginia. *Henry James's American Girl: The Embroidery on the Canvas.* Madison: University of Wisconsin Press, 1984.

Fussell, Edwin. "Fitzgerald's Brave New World." In *Critical Essays on "Tender Is the Night."* Ed. Milton R. Stern. Critical Essays on American Literature. Boston: G. K. Hall, 1986.

Gaess, Roger, and Wyatt James, eds. *Expatriate Review* 1–4 (1971–74).

Gates, Henry Louis, Jr. " 'Authenticity,' or the Lesson of Little Tree." *New York Times Book Review* (24 November 1991).

———. "Authority, (White) Power, and the (Black) Critic." Special issue of *Cultural Critique* 7 (Fall 1987).

———. "Criticism in the Jungle." In *Black Literature and Literary Theory.* Ed. Henry Louis Gates, Jr. New York: Methuen, 1984.

———. "Tell Me, Sir . . . What *Is* Black Literature?" Special issue of *PMLA* 105.1 (January 1990).

———, ed. *"Race," Writing, and Difference.* Chicago: University of Chicago Press, 1986.

Gayle, Addison. "The Function of Black Literature at the Present Time." In *The Black Aesthetic.* Ed. Addison Gayle. New York: Doubleday, 1971.

Gibson, Donald B. "The Politics of Ellison and Baldwin." In *The Politics of Twentieth-Century Writers.* Ed. George Panichas. New York: Hawthorne, 1971.

Girard, René. *Deceit, Desire, and the Novel: Self and Other in Literary Structure.* Trans. Yvonne Freccero. Baltimore: Johns Hopkins University Press, 1965.

———. *Violence and the Sacred.* Trans. Patrick Gregory. Baltimore: Johns Hopkins University Press, 1977.

Godden, Richard. "Some Slight Shifts in the Manner of the Novel of Manners." In *Henry James: Fiction as History.* Ed. Ian F. A. Bell. London: Vision, 1984.

Golab, Caroline. *Immigrant Destinations.* Philadelphia: Temple University Press, 1977.

Goldberg, David Theo, ed. *Anatomy of Racism.* Minneapolis: University of Minnesota Press, 1990.

Goldmann, Lucien. *Towards a Sociology of the Novel.* Trans. Alan Sheridan. London: Tavistock, 1975.

Goldstein, Richard. " 'Go the Way Your Blood Beats': An Interview with James Baldwin." *Village Voice* (26 June 1984).

Greenberg, David F. *The Construction of Homosexuality.* Chicago: University of Chicago Press, 1988.

Grund, Francis. *Aristocracy in America.* New York: Harper, 1959.

Handlin, Oscar. *The Uprooted.* Boston: Little, Brown, 1951.

Haney, Lynn. *Naked at the Feast: A Biography of Josephine Baker.* New York: Dodd, Mead, 1981.

Hansen, Marcus Lee. *The Atlantic Migration, 1607–1860.* Cambridge: Harvard University Press, 1940.

Hirsch, E. D., Jr. *Cultural Literacy: What Every American Needs to Know.* Boston: Houghton, 1987.

James, Henry. *The American Scene.* 1907. Ed. Leon Edel. Bloomington: Indiana University Press, 1968.

————. *The Art of the Novel.* Ed. R. P. Blackmur. New York: Scribner's, 1934.

————. "The Beast in the Jungle." In *Selected Fiction.* Ed. Leon Edel. New York: Dutton, 1964.

————. *The Complete Notebooks.* Ed. Leon Edel and Lyall H. Powers. New York: Oxford University Press, 1987.

————. *Daisy Miller.* In *Selected Fiction.* Ed. Leon Edel. New York: Dutton, 1964.

————. *Hawthorne.* 1879. Reprint. Ithaca: Cornell University Press, 1956.

————. *The Letters.* Ed. Percy Lubbock. New York: Scribner's, 1920.

————. *The Portrait of a Lady.* Ed. Robert E. Bamburg. New York: Norton, 1975.

Jameson, Frederic. *The Political Unconscious: Narrative as a Socially Symbolic Act.* Ithaca: Cornell University Press, 1981.

Jardine, Alice, and Paul Smith, eds. *Men in Feminism.* London: Methuen, 1987.

Johnson, Barbara. *A World of Difference.* Baltimore: Johns Hopkins University Press, 1987.

Jordan, Winthrop D. *White over Black: American Attitudes toward the Negro, 1550–1812.* Chapel Hill: University of North Carolina Press, 1968.

Kellogg, Stuart, ed. *Literary Visions of Homosexuality.* Special issue of *Journal of Homosexuality* 8, nos. 3–4 (Spring–Summer 1983).

Kinnamon, Kenneth, ed. *James Baldwin: A Collection of Critical Essays.* Englewood Cliffs, N.J.: Prentice-Hall, 1974.

Knapp, Bettina. *Exile and the Writer: Exoteric and Esoteric Experiences, a Jungian Approach.* University Park: Pennsylvania State University Press, 1991.

Koestenbaum, Wayne. *Double Talk: The Erotics of Male Literary Collaboration.* New York: Routledge, 1989.

Kolodny, Annette. *The Lay of the Land: Metaphor as Experience and History in American Life and Letters.* Chapel Hill: University of North Carolina Press, 1975.

Kovel, Joel. *White Racism: A Psychohistory.* New York: Random, 1970.

Leeming, David Adams. "An Interview with James Baldwin on Henry James." *Henry James Review* 8 (Fall 1986).

Le Vot, André. *F. Scott Fitzgerald.* Trans. William Byron. New York: Doubleday, 1983.

Lewis, David Levering. *When Harlem Was in Vogue.* New York: Knopf, 1981.

Lukács, Georg. *Essays on Realism.* Ed. Rodney Livingstone. Trans. David Fernbach. Cambridge: MIT Press, 1980.

MacShane, Frank, ed. *The American in Europe: A Collection of Impressions by Americans Written from the Seventeenth Century to the Present.* New York: Dutton, 1965.

McCarthy, Harold T. *The Expatriate Perspective: American Novelists and the Idea of America.* Rutherford: Fairleigh Dickinson, 1974.

McCarthy, Mary. *Occasional Prose.* New York: Harcourt, 1985.

Martin, Wallace. *Recent Theories of Narrative.* Ithaca: Cornell University Press, 1986.

Mayfied, Sara. *Exiles from Paradise.* New York: Delacorte, 1971.

Mellow, James R. *Invented Lives: F. Scott and Zelda Fitzgerald.* Boston: Houghton, 1984.

Miller, D. A. *The Novel and the Police.* Berkeley and Los Angeles: University of California Press, 1988.

Moi, Toril. *Sexual/Textual Politics: Feminist Literary Theory.* London: Methuen, 1985.

Morrison, Toni. *Playing in the Dark: Whiteness and the Literary Imagination.* Cambridge: Harvard University Press, 1992.

Newman, Charles. "The Lesson of the Master: Henry James and James Baldwin." *Yale Review* 56 (October 1966): 45–59.

O'Daniel, Therman B., ed. *James Baldwin: A Critical Evaluation.* Washington, D.C.: Howard University Press, 1977.

Phillips, Caryl. *The European Tribe.* London: Faber, 1987.

Pieterse, Jan Nederveen. *White on Black: Images of Africa and Blacks in Western Popular Culture*. New Haven: Yale University Press, 1992.

Porter, Horace. *Stealing the Fire: The Art and Protest of James Baldwin*. Middletown, Conn.: Wesleyan University Press, 1989.

Putnam, Samuel. *Paris Was Our Mistress: Memoirs of a Lost and Found Generation*. New York: Viking, 1947.

Rampersad, Arnold. "Slavery and the Literary Imagination: Du Bois's *The Souls of Black Folk*." In *Slavery and the Literary Imagination*. Ed. Deborah E. McDowell and Arnold Rampersad. Baltimore: Johns Hopkins University Press, 1989.

Said, Edward. *The World, the Text, and the Critic*. Cambridge: Harvard University Press, 1983.

Scholes, Robert. *Fabulation and Metafiction*. Urbana: University of Illinois Press, 1979.

Sedgwick, Eve Kosofsky. "The Beast in the Closet: James and the Writing of Homosexual Panic." In *Epistemology of the Closet*. Berkeley and Los Angeles: University of California Press, 1990.

————. *Between Men: English Literature and Male Homosocial Desire*. New York: Columbia University Press, 1985.

Seidler, Victor. *Rediscovering Masculinity: Reason, Language, and Sexuality*. London: Routledge, 1989.

Smith, Henry Nash. *Democracy and the Novel: Popular Resistance to Classic American Writers*. New York: Oxford University Press, 1978.

Spender, Stephen. *Love-Hate Relations: English and American Sensibilities*. New York: Random, 1974.

Steiner, George. "The Archives of Eden." *Salmagundi* 50 (1980): 61–80.

Steiner, Wendy. "Review of *Playing in the Dark*." *New York Times Book Review* (5 April 1992).

Stowe, Harriet Beecher. *Uncle Tom's Cabin*. 1852. Reprint. Toronto: Bantam, 1981.

Summers, Claude J. *Gay Fictions, Wilde to Stonewall: Studies in a Male Homosexual Literary Tradition*. New York: Continuum, 1990.

Tompkins, Jane. *Sensational Designs: The Cultural Work of American Fiction, 1790–1860*. New York: Oxford University Press, 1985.

Torgovnick, Marianna. *Gone Primitive: Savage Intellects, Modern Lives*. Chicago: University of Chicago Press, 1990.

Trilling, Lionel. *The Liberal Imagination*. New York: Viking, 1950.

Wasserstrom, William. *Heiress of All the Ages*. Minneapolis: University of Minnesota Press, 1959.

Weatherby, W. J. *James Baldwin: Artist on Fire*. New York: Dell, 1989.

Wegelin, Christof. *The Image of Europe in Henry James*. Dallas: Southern Methodist University Press, 1958.

West, Cornel. *Race Matters*. Boston: Beacon, 1993.

An Actor Prepares (Stanislavsky), 131
Adorno, Theodor, 48–49
Aeschylus, 105
Africa, 7, 64, 95, 98, 102–3, 105–6
African Americans, 73, 76; as charac-
    ters in African American texts,
    132, 135–39; as characters in
    white texts, 23, 24, 63–65; Fitz-
    gerald's views of, 43, 45, 56;
    James on, 113–15, 117–18; nego-
    tiations of, with white culture,
    4–5, 15, 17–19, 21–25, 73–74,
    77, 80–91, 95–108; as Other, 31,
    99–101; white characters in texts
    by, 25, 70–73, 124. *See also* Exiles
    (black); Harlem Renaissance;
    Race; Racism; Slavery; *Names of
    specific African Americans*
"Alas, Poor Richard" (Baldwin), 72
The Ambassadors (James), 30
America, 9, 94, 112; history of racial
    oppression in, 26–30, 101–4,
    131; as lacking in civilization, 10,
    12, 36–40, 47–53, 56, 109; as un-
    inhabitable, 8–9, 52, 53, 109. *See
    also* New York City; South

The American Scene (James), 12, 40,
    49–50, 109–21, 126
Another Country (Baldwin), 6, 127–42;
    heterosexuality in, 130, 131–33;
    homosexuality in, 75, 82, 130–
    31; James's influence on, 17–18,
    127
Antidemocratic views. *See* Democracy
Art, 12–13, 36–38, 55, 63. *See also*
    Novel(s)
Assimilationism. *See* Universalism
Auerbach, Nina, 37

Bach, Johann Sebastian, 105
Bachelors, 5–6, 121
Baker, Houston, 14, 43, 44
Bakhtin, M. M., 38, 145n8
Baldwin, James: critics on, 97, 120,
    128; depictions of racism by,
    25–30, 121–26, 137, 142; Euro-
    centrism of, 95, 96, 109; as exile,
    7–8, 10, 18, 94, 95; handling of
    homosexual themes by, 7, 8,
    25–30, 35, 70–91, 96, 128–31,
    142; homosexuality of, 79–80,
    95, 96, 129, 130; ideology in

works by, 10, 14, 70–91, 95–96;
interviews with, 15, 30, 79–80,
97; James's influence on, 3, 7, 15,
17–21, 24, 25, 30, 73, 77, 80–91,
107, 119, 121, 131, 136; on race,
20, 98–108, 121–25; on reading
James, 19; transgressions of
boundaries in works by, 6, 134;
as universalist, 21, 73, 79, 95–96,
104, 123–25
Baraka, Amiri, 97
"The Beast in the Jungle" (James), 7,
17, 23, 24, 80–86, 88–91, 128
Beethoven, Ludwig von, 105
Bell, Ian F. A., 18
Benstock, Shari, 9
Bergman, David, 74, 128, 133
Between Men (Sedgwick), 84
Bigsby, C. W. E., 5, 7–8
Birth of a Nation (film), 65
Bisexuality, 6, 128, 133, 137, 140
Black Muslims, 122
Bloom, Allan, 70
Bloom, Harold, 20
Blues, 136
Boelhower, William, 110, 115–16
Bone, Robert, 70
Boundaries. *See* Class; Gender; Race;
Sexual orientation
Breeding, 42–45, 59. *See also* Class; Re-
production
Broe, Mary Lynn, 9
Bruccoli, Matthew, 49
Bryan, Gertrude, 13

Callahan, John, 56–58, 60, 66, 67
Camus, Albert, 7
Canon, 8, 11; African Americans' ne-
gotiations with, 4–5, 7–8, 15,
22–24; Baldwin's admission to,
96–98, 109; Baldwin's new, 131;
gay, 72, 128; James's role in, 18,
109; outsiders' reading of, 4, 14,
15, 105–7; whites' domination of,
21, 105–7. *See also* Western traditions
Capitalism, 9, 60–62, 111, 122
Carpenter, Humphrey, 10
Castration, 29–30, 82
Celibates, 5–6
Cendrars, Blaise, 131
Chartres Cathedral, 105
Chestnutt, Charles, 21
Chinese, 117, 118
City of Richmond (ship), 5, 36, 40
Civil War, 36, 40, 55, 65–66, 114, 118
Civilization: exclusion as basis of,
47–52, 64, 110–12; fears about
decline of, 5, 9, 14, 44, 45, 47,
56, 58, 61; "masculine" women as
threat to, 61–62; and racism, 21;
women as factor in preserving, 9,
12, 13–14, 37–39, 41–42, 47,
50–51, 53, 55, 57–60
Claire, Ina, 13
Class: and Baldwin, 19, 126; Fitzger-
ald's views on, 3, 9, 55, 56, 59,
63; and James, 3, 9, 19, 35–36,
39–40, 47, 53, 112–23, 126;
readers', 20
Cleaver, Eldridge, 72, 73, 77, 95, 96,
104
Commodification, 41–42, 52, 58–59,
61, 90–91, 130, 134–35, 139,
140
Commuter imagery, 15, 94
Conversations with James Baldwin (ed.
Standley and Pratt), 97

Cooper, James Fenimore, 10, 11, 118
Cowley, Malcolm, 8–9, 11, 68–69,
    100, 121
The Crack-up (Fitzgerald), 12, 13, 58
The Crisis of the Negro Intellectual (Cruse),
    11, 95–96
Critics: on Baldwin, 97, 120, 128–30,
    141; depoliticizing by, 49,
    52–53, 56–57, 70, 119–20, 128;
    failure of, to analyze ideological
    elements in Fitzgerald's works,
    49, 52–53, 56–57; failure of, to
    analyze ideological elements in
    James's works, 23–24, 38, 71,
    113–14, 119–20; on Hurston,
    124–25
Cruse, Harold, 11, 95–96

Daisy Miller (James), 5, 24, 45, 47, 57;
    as influence on *The Great Gatsby*,
    30, 35–40, 46, 53, 54
Dante Alighieri, 105
Davis, Sammy, Jr., 123
De Lauretis, Teresa, 129
Democracy, 9, 38–40, 47–54, 122,
    123
Didion, Joan, 50
Differences magazine, 129
"The Discovery of What It Means to
    Be an American" (Baldwin), 17,
    20, 109, 112, 126
Drag, 13–14, 76, 133
Dreiser, Theodore, 118
D'Souza, Dinesh, 70
Du Bois, W. E. B., 21, 114
Dupee, F. W., 38

Earnest, Ernest, 11
"East River, Downtown" (Baldwin),
    109, 123–25

Edel, Leon, 113, 115–16
Eliot, T. S., 45
Emancipation Proclamation, 88
Engendering Men (ed. Boone), 120
Epistemology of the Closet (Sedgwick), 71,
    84, 119, 120
Ethnic populations: Baldwin's refer-
    ences to, 140; white exiles' views
    of, 9, 11, 35, 48–49, 55, 112–19,
    126. *See also* African Americans
Europe, 112; meaning of, to exiles,
    5–12, 37–39, 45, 51, 53, 67, 94,
    98–108, 110, 125–26, 131. *See
    also* Switzerland
"Everybody's Protest Novel" (Bald-
    win), 72
Exclusion. *See* Privacy
Exiles (black): experience of, 11, 20,
    98–104, 106–8, 125–26, 128;
    white exiles' influence on, 3, 7–8,
    18, 98–99, 121–23; in white
    texts, 64–65. *See also* Civilization;
    Exiles (white)
Exile's Return (Cowley), 8–9
Exiles (white): and black exiles,
    64–65, 101; Cowley's analysis of,
    8–10, 100; filiative problems of,
    5–6, 121; ideology of, 7, 9, 11,
    53; as influence on Baldwin, 3,
    18, 98–99; texts about, 71. *See
    also* Civilization; Exiles (black)
The Expatriate Perspective (McCarthy), 10
Expatriots and Patriots (Earnest), 11

Fabre, Michel, 10, 65
Faulkner, William, 22
Fauset, Jessie, 7, 65
"Fifth Avenue, Uptown" (Baldwin),
    109, 121–23

Filiation, 5–6, 121
Film(s), 65, 76; Fitzgerald on, 12–13, 56, 58–60
Fisher, Philip, 118
Fitch, Noel Riley, 10
Fitzgerald, F. Scott: emphasis on boundaries in works by, 5–6; on films, 12–13, 56, 58–60; ideology of, 9, 10, 12, 14, 31, 36–45, 47–53, 55–69; influence of James on, 9, 12, 19, 40–54; as white exile, 7, 11, 98
Flaubert, Gustave, 22, 143n13
Ford, Ford Madox, 94
Forms: African Americans' uses of, 73, 106, 128; James's, 18, 24, 25, 118. See also Novel(s)
France, 7, 11–12, 53, 59, 67, 68, 74, 122, 125–26
"Freaks and the American Ideal of Manhood" (Baldwin), 97–98
Frontier references, 55, 67–68
Fussell, Edwin, 65

Gaiety Transfigured (Bergman), 74, 128
Gates, Henry Louis, Jr., 4–5, 21–22, 70, 97–98, 106
Gausse's Hotel des Étrangers, 53
Gay theory, 128–30, 141. See also Homosexuality
Gayle, Addison, 95, 98, 104, 106
Gender, 3, 115, 120, 130. See also Gender roles; Men; Women
Gender roles, 61–62, 75–76, 79, 85–88, 133, 137, 142. See also Drag shows
Genet, Jean, 131
Geniuses Together (Carpenter), 10
Genre. See Forms

Genteel tradition (James's), 35–38
Gide, André, 27, 130
Giovanni's Room (Baldwin), 6–8, 17, 24, 70–91, 128, 129, 136, 141
Giovanni's Room (Philadelphia bookstore), 70–71
Girard, René, 46
Go Tell It on the Mountain (Baldwin), 72, 76, 98
Godden, Richard, 41–42
"Going to Meet the Man" (Baldwin), 15, 17–31, 35, 130, 142
The Golden Bowl (James), 40, 87, 127
The Great Gatsby (Fitzgerald), 5, 13, 31, 35, 37, 40–55, 60, 65, 74
Griffith, D. W., 12–13, 65

Handy, W. C., 136
Harlem Renaissance, 11, 43
Hawthorne, Nathaniel, 10, 11
Hawthorne (James), 17
Heiress of All the Ages (Wasserstrom), 38–39
Hemingway, Ernest, 7, 10, 11, 127
"Henry James and James Baldwin" (Powers), 21
Henry James Review, 30
"Here Be Dragons" (Baldwin), 97–98
Heterosexuality, 6, 141–42; and homophobia, 91; impact of, on homosexuals, 75, 78, 82, 89–90, 121, 130, 131–33, 140; and marriage, 87, 127, 132–33. See also Gender roles; Homophobia; Reproduction
Hierarchies. See Class; Gender; Race; Sexual orientation
Hirsch, E. D., 70
Hollywood. See Film(s)

Homophobia, 72, 74–78, 91, 95–96, 129–30; and racism, 6–7. *See also* Sex and race

"Homosexual panic," 27–30, 35, 46, 80–81, 120, 128

Homosexuality: Baldwin's, 79–80, 95, 96, 129, 130; Baldwin's depiction of, 7, 8, 25–30, 35, 70–91, 96, 128–31, 142; critics' references to authors', 24, 71–73, 97, 119–20, 128; Fitzgerald's fear of, 61; as form of exile, 121, 128; impact of heterosexual models on, 75, 78, 82, 89–90, 121, 130, 131–33, 140; and patriarchy, 84–85, 139–40; relationship building in, 129, 131–32, 138–39, 141; as subtext in James's work, 5–6, 24–25, 36, 45, 46, 53, 71, 73, 80–86, 89–91, 113, 115, 117–21, 128. *See also* Homophobia; "Homosexual panic"; Sex and race; Sexual orientation

Hotel imagery, 47–53

House imagery, 47–52, 62–63, 111–12. *See also* Room imagery

The House of Mirth (Wharton), 117

"How It Feels to Be Colored Me" (Hurston), 124

Hughes, Langston, 65

Hurston, Zora Neale, 124–25

Illusions of a Nation (Callahan), 56–58

Immigration. *See* Ethnic populations; Nativism

Imperialism, 55

"In Another Country" (Hemingway), 127

Incest, 60–61, 142

Indians of North America, 31, 67–68, 118

Individualism, 21, 79–80

Industrialization, 55. *See also* Urbanization

Influence: of James on Baldwin, 3, 7, 15, 17–21, 24, 25, 30, 73, 77, 80–91, 107, 119, 121, 131, 136; of James on Fitzgerald, 9, 12, 19, 40–54; theories of, 20

Ingram, Angela, 9

Intertextuality. *See* Influence

Italians, 113, 115–17

Jackson, Shirley, 28

James, Henry, 22, 49–50; and class, 3, 9, 19, 35–36, 39–40, 47, 53, 112–23, 126; critics' failure to analyze elements in works by, 23–24, 38, 71, 113–14, 119–20; emphasis on boundaries in works by, 5–6, 110–12; as exile, 10, 109, 144*n*13; ideology of, 3, 9, 10, 14, 18–19, 24, 30–31, 37–39, 109–22, 125–26; as influence on Baldwin, 3, 7, 15, 17–21, 24, 25, 30, 73, 77, 80–91, 107, 119, 121, 131, 136; as influence on Fitzgerald, 9, 12, 19, 40–54; treatment of homosexual desire by, 5–6, 24–25, 36, 45, 46, 53, 71, 73, 80–86, 89–91, 113, 115, 117–21, 128. *See also* Forms

James, William, 112

James Baldwin: The Legacy (ed. Troupe), 96–98

Jazz, 48–49

Jehlen, Myra, 115, 119

Jews: Fitzgerald's view of, 42–43, 45;
James's views of, 9, 113, 115,
117, 118
Johnson, Barbara, 124–25
Joyce, James, 101

Keats, John, 58
Klinkowitz, Jerome, 143n13
Kovel, Joel, 28–29

Lady Barbarina (James), 17–18, 127
Language, 105–6
Lanier, Sidney, 63
Larsen, Nella, 7
Latinos, 76
Le Vot, André, 57
Leonardo da Vinci, 105
"The Lesson of the Master" (Newman), 20–21
Lewis, David Levering, 115
Lincoln, Abraham, 88
Little Boy Blue, 13
Livingston, Jennie, 76
"Lost generation," 10, 11, 18, 100
"The Lottery" (Jackson), 28
Lynchings, 26–30

McCarthy, Harold, 10
McKay, Claude, 7, 65
MacLeish, Archibald, 11
Madame Bovary (Flaubert), 143n13
Madeleine (Gide), 27
Mainstream. *See* Marginal
"The Male Prison" (Baldwin), 27, 130
Malinowski, Bronislaw, 107
Marginal, 4, 15, 91, 106, 121, 129
Marriage, 87, 127, 132–33. *See also* Relationship building
Martin, Wallace, 10

Matthiessen, F. O., 113
Mead, Margaret, 107
Melville, Herman, 10, 22
Men: Baldwin's portrayal of white, 72,
74–83, 88, 90–91, 128, 136;
James's and Fitzgerald's view of,
9, 13. *See also* Gender; Gender
roles
Men in Feminism (ed. Jardine and
Smith), 120
Michelangelo, 105
Mirror imagery, 81–82, 141
Miscegenation, 43, 52, 96, 104–5,
132. *See also* Sex and race
Misogyny. *See* Sexism
Modernism and the Harlem Renaissance
(Baker), 43–44
Modernists, 6, 14, 44, 110
Moi, Toril, 14–15
Monoculturalism. *See* Universalism
Morrison, Toni, 4–5, 22–25, 97
Mosby, John Singleton, 65–66

Native Son (Wright), 17, 72–73, 131
Nativism, 9, 67, 112–21. *See also* Ethnic populations
New York City: Baldwin's view of,
109, 121–24, 126; Fitzgerald's
view of, 12, 13; James's view of,
12, 109–11, 113, 115, 117–18,
125
Newman, Charles, 20–21
Newport (Rhode Island), 49–50, 53
"Notes of a Native Son" (Baldwin),
17, 98
Notes of a Son and Brother (James), 17
Novel(s): Bahktin on, 145n9; exiles'
use of, 10, 38; Fitzgerald's fears
about, 13, 56; as way of perceiving Other, 133–34. *See also* Forms

"Ode to a Nightingale" (Keats), 58
Orphans, 5–6
Other, 30–31, 99–101, 133–34. See
    also African Americans; Ethnic
    populations; Indians; Jews

Paglia, Camille, 70
Paris. See France
Paris Is Burning (Livingston), 76
Paris Was Our Mistress (Putnam), 11–12
Philomel, 45
Pieterse, Jan Nederveen, 56
Playboy magazine, 97–98
Playing in the Dark (Morrison), 4–5,
    22–24, 31
Plaza Hotel, 52
Porter, Horace, 21, 73
The Portrait of a Lady (James), 19, 30
Powers, Lyall, 21
The Princess Casamassima (James), 30
Privacy (exclusion), 47–52, 64,
    110–12, 134
Proust, Marcel, 131
Putnam, Samuel, 11–12

The Quaker Girl, 13

Race: Baldwin's views on, 20, 27–28,
    70–72, 98–108, 121–25; break-
    down of binarisms of, 6, 125–26,
    132–33; critics' failure to deal
    with authors', 23–24, 49, 71;
    Fitzgerald's views on, 3, 9, 12,
    42–45, 52, 63–69; James's views
    on, 3, 9, 23–24, 36, 38, 53, 113;
    readers', 4–5, 20; reading for,
    115; writing about, 120. See also
    African Americans; Ethnic popu-
    lations; Racism; Sex and race;
    Whites

Race Matters (West), 28, 29
"Race," Writing, and Difference (ed.
    Gates), 120
Racine, Jean, 105
Racism: Baldwin's depiction of, 25–30,
    121–26, 137, 142; and civiliza-
    tion, 21; Fitzgerald's, 9, 12,
    42–45, 52, 63–69; and homo-
    phobia, 6–7, 119–20; James's,
    18–19, 116, 119–20; of white ex-
    iles, 7, 9. See also Critics; Nativ-
    ism; Race
Rampersad, Arnold, 114
Rape, 29, 46, 68; metaphor of, 51, 97,
    105–6
Reconstruction period, 36
Relationship building, 5–6, 121; be-
    tween heterosexuals, 134–35; be-
    tween homosexuals, 129, 131–
    32, 138–39, 141
Rembrandt van Rijn, 105
Reproduction, 5–6, 96, 118, 121, 129
Revolution, 122–23, 136–37
Rising Tide of Color against White Suprem-
    acy (Stoddard), 44, 65
La Rive Noire (Fabre), 10, 65
Room imagery, 78–79

Said, Edward, 6, 144n20
Sartre, Jean-Paul, 7
Scholes, Robert, 133–34
The Second Black Renaissance (Bigsby), 5
Sedgwick, Eve Kosofsky, 27, 71,
    84–86, 88–89, 119–21
Sex and race: in Baldwin's works, 6–7,
    25–30, 35, 70–76, 88, 97–98,
    102; in Fitzgerald's works, 52; in
    James's works, 24–25, 35–36. See
    also Miscegenation; Race; Sexual
    orientation

Sexism (misogyny), 84; in Baldwin's
  works, 77, 131, 139–40, 142; in
  Fitzgerald's works, 46, 56, 62
Sexual desire, 3, 71. *See also* Bisexual-
  ity; Heterosexuality; Homosexu-
  ality
Sexual orientation, 6, 120, 130. *See also*
  Bisexuality; Heterosexuality; Ho-
  mosexuality
Sexual/Textual Politics (Moi), 14–15
Shakespeare, William, 105
The Shame of the Cities (Steffens),
  116–17
Shelley, Mary, 22
Sinatra, Frank, 123
Skyscrapers, 111–12
Slavery, 115; Baldwin's allusions to,
  88, 102–3; Fitzgerald's references
  to, 63–66; James's views on, 9,
  113, 114, 118
Slouching towards Bethlehem (Didion), 50
Smith, Bessie, 136
Sontag, Susan, 13
Soul on Ice (Cleaver), 72, 96
The Souls of Black Folk (Du Bois), 21,
  114
The South, 40, 65–66, 113–14
Spain, 7
Spengler, Oswald, 147n6
Stealing the Fire (Porter), 21
Steffens, Lincoln, 116
Stein, Gertrude, 7, 10
Steiner, Wendy, 24
Stoddard, Lothrop, 44, 65
Stowe, Harriet Beecher, 20, 55,
  63–64, 68, 118
"Stranger in the Village" (Baldwin), 7,
  17, 52, 98–104, 106–8, 131;
  Western canon in, 22, 98, 105,

106–7; white-black relations in,
  8, 27–28, 95–108
Summers, Claude, 71, 72
Switzerland, 54, 98–104, 106–8
Sylvia Beach and the Lost Generation
  (Fitch), 10

Taboos, 71, 73. *See also* Homosexuality
Tar Baby (Morrison), 25
Tea parties, 19, 30, 48
"Tell Me, Sir . . . What *Is* Black Litera-
  ture?" (Gates), 97–98
Tender Is the Night (Fitzgerald), 13, 31,
  53, 54–69, 98
Tiresias, 45
Tompkins, Jane, 63–64
Torgovnick, Marianna, 107–8
Trilling, Lionel, 38, 52–53
The Turn of the Screw (James), 30

Uncle Tom's Cabin (Stowe), 63
Uncle Tom's Children (Wright), 72
Universalism, 21, 73, 79, 95–98, 104,
  120, 123–25, 128
Urbanization, 118. *See also* Industrial-
  ization

Village Voice, 79–80

Waldorf Astoria Hotel, 47, 110
Wasserstrom, William, 38–39, 41
The Waste Land (Eliot), 45
Weatherby, W. J., 19
West, Cornel, 28, 29
Western traditions, 7, 14, 98, 105,
  106–8. *See also* Canon; Critics;
  Europe; Modernism
Wharton, Edith, 117
What Maisie Knew (James), 23, 24

When Harlem Was in Vogue (Levering), 115

White Racism (Kovel), 28–29

White texts: black readers' negotiations with, 4–5, 15, 22–24; influence of, on black texts, 7–8. *See also* Canon; Critics; *Titles of works by Fitzgerald and James*

Whites: African American portrayals of, 25–27, 70–83, 90–91, 124, 128, 131–36, 139–42; as savages, 107–8

Wilson, Edmund, 66–67

The Wings of the Dove (James), 30, 131

Women: Baldwin's portrayal of, 75, 77, 83, 86–88, 131–36, 139–42; as civilizing factor, 9, 12, 13–14, 37–39, 41–42, 47, 50–51, 53, 55, 57–60; invisibility of, in male texts, 84; "masculine," as threat to civilization, 61–62; scholars' failure to analyze Fitzgerald's treatment of, 23–24; as sexual threat, 41–42, 45–46, 111. *See also* Gender; Gender roles; Sexism

Women of the Left Bank (Benstock), 9

Women's Writing in Exile (Broe and Ingram), 9–10

Working class. *See* Class; Ethnic populations

Wright, Richard, 7, 97; as influence on Baldwin, 17, 20, 72–73, 136